for
Better
for Worse

for Better for Worse

A light-hearted guide to wedded bliss

Jane Fearnley-Whittingstall

Illustrations by Stephanie von Reiswitz

First published in 2010 by

Short Books
3A Exmouth House
Pine Street
EC1R 0JH

10 9 8 7 6 5 4 3 2 1

A CIP catalogue record for this book is available from the British Library.

ISBN 978-1-904977-76-6

Printed in Great Britain by Clays, Suffolk

Illustration © Stephanie von Reiswitz

For Rob, of course

CONTENTS

INTRODUCTION

The most wonderful of all things in life is the discovery of another human being with whom one's relationship has a growing depth, beauty and joy as the years increase. This inner progressiveness of love between two human beings is a most marvellous thing; it cannot be found by looking for it or by passionately wishing for it. It is a sort of divine accident, and the most wonderful of all things in life.

Sir Hugh Walpole (1884-1941)

When I was halfway through writing this book, my husband and I went out to dinner. The man sitting next to me asked me what I was working on. 'It's called *For Better for Worse*,' I said. 'It's about marriage and how to survive it – a humorous look at the joys and pains of married life…'

'So you think marriage is a good thing?' he asked.

The question took me by surprise. Ever since my mother read me the story of Cinderella, I had assumed that 'to get married and live happily ever after' was what life was all about. And in every important respect I have never really doubted it.

We live in a changing world, and today couples are as likely to make their marriage vows on a palm-fringed beach, in a medieval castle or, less romantically, at a country club or register office, as in a church. They've also probably lived together before deciding to marry. But some things never change: when men and women fall in love, they still choose to spend their lives together, and most couples still exchange the traditional solemn promises, with friends and families gathered around to support them.

> *For better, for worse*
> *For richer, for poorer*
> *In sickness and in health*
> *Until death us do part.*

The promises are, of course, idealistic to the point of being unrealistic, and certainly easier to make than to keep. We might think, when we embark on the adventure of marriage, that loving and cherishing would come easily. Not a bit of it. Even when everything's working out for better rather than worse and we're richer than we ever hoped, and in the best of health, as the novelty of shared domesticity wears off, there will be times when we wonder what on earth we've let ourselves in for. However madly in love two people are, 'Until death…' can occasionally seem like a very long time indeed.

So do I think marriage is a good thing? Heavens, yes. But I don't think it's easy. I'm not a marriage guidance expert. But I have been there, done that. Rob and I have been happily married for 47 years. We've been through the usual ups and downs, and I've been an analytic, as well as sympathetic, observer of other people's marriages over three generations: my parents', my own and my children's. But above all, for this book, I've been helped by numerous friends, relations and strangers, many of whom have been astonishingly frank about the 'for worse' aspects as well as the 'for better'.

This book is intended not so much as a 'how to' manual as an entertaining and informative companion, to be dipped into and pondered over at will. It is a collective testimony of experience — a mixture of past and present voices and extracts from literary and historic sources.

Luckily for us, generations of people have written wisely, astutely and wittily about marriage. And the interviews I did with people over a vast age range were remarkably eye-opening and strangely heartening. They remind us that we are not alone: for centuries husbands and wives have found it hard to keep their marriage vows to the letter. Not to mention various other important but unwritten commandments such as:

Thou shalt not have the last word

Thou shalt put the rubbish out even though
it's not thy turn
Thou shalt always be nice to thy mother-in-law

When we consider the hectic demands of modern exitence – two independent people balancing busy jobs with domestic life, and the need to keep in touch with their wider families and friends – it seems a miracle that marriage has survived in any shape or form at all. On weekdays a young couple hardly catch sight of each other before rushing to work, and in the evening they might spend only moments together cooking a meal before slumping exhausted in front of the TV. At weekends there might be a spot of cleaning, a supermarket shop, the dry cleaner's and a bit of DIY, before Sunday lunch at the in-laws and a trip to the pub with friends.

All of which doesn't leave much time for thinking about the relationship. When I asked couples what qualities they valued in each other, many said how much they enjoyed just sitting down and thinking about it. Their answers were heart-warming. Very few were impressed by good looks or style. Both men and women used words like 'honesty', 'integrity', 'loyalty' and 'tolerance'. Gentleness and kindness were highly valued. One wife wrote, 'My husband is the kindest man in the world'; another, 'He is unselfish and considerate and shows thoughtfulness for other people'; 'He pushes me to do things for myself, gives me confidence'; 'He's totally supportive'.

That's all very encouraging, but the path of true love, as

we all know, does not always run quite so smooth. When people live in close proximity, however considerate they are, they will find they irritate each other more, not less, as time goes by. If our partner is by no means perfect, neither are we, and the people I asked had no difficulty in identifying their own annoying characteristics once they started thinking about them. Marriage tells us as much about ourselves as it does about others.

What was most marked, if perhaps predictable, was how much more voluble and fluent in their complaints women were than men. Most wives, asked to write down their husbands' annoying characteristics, came up with a long list.

Men seem to be either less irritable, or more reticent about sharing their views. Some husbands were even generous enough to give a positive slant to qualities that might seem negative to others. An ostensibly bossy wife is praised for being organised, and for 'her spirit of independence'. Few women see things so positively, though one said that the time her husband spent in the pub or playing sport was a small price to pay for his extrovert outlook on life, which made him such good company and fun to be with.

Accusations made with equal frequency by men and women included stubbornness ('She's always right!' and 'He's so pig-headed – thinks he knows it all!'), indecision, and forgetfulness ('She forgets important dates'; 'His failure to communicate about day-to-day events drives me up the wall').

The negative aspects of life as a couple are not shirked in this book. They are highlighted alongside the positive, with quotations from literature, history and even internet chatrooms. A fascinating picture emerges of how people negotiate what is probably the most important relationship of their lives — how they behave towards each other when they are alone together or out and about, and how they get along with each other's family and friends; what problems occur for richer and for poorer, as money turns out to be the biggest cause of marital rows; and even how they behave in the sickroom.

I look at the challenge of staying together as a marriage develops, and chart the flashpoints and threats. The delicate issues of monogamy and adultery are reviewed and discussed, including the seven-year itch and its temptations, and the agonies of jealousy. In spite of the difficulties, nearly all the couples I spoke to agreed that their marriage has kept them happy and sane in a sometimes mad world. Certainly, when our cherished goals bob out of reach like a beach ball carried on the tide, it helps to see the funny side. Married life, with its inevitable flaws and foibles, is best treated as a sitcom rather than a Greek tragedy — Jack and Vera Duckworth are not very romantic role models, but they beat Agamemnon and Clytemnestra.

Above all, this book is intended as a celebration of the institution of marriage: a source of closeness, comfort, mutual support, moments of great joy, uncanny telepathy, deep contentment and much laughter and companionship. What's more, the pleasures increase as the years go by. As

INTRODUCTION

André Maurois wrote: 'A happy marriage is a long conversation that always seems too short.'

THE OWL AND THE PUSSY-CAT

The Owl and the Pussy-cat went to sea
In a beautiful pea-green boat.
They took some honey, and plenty of money
Wrapped up in a five pound note.

The Owl looked up to the stars above
And sang to a small guitar
'O Lovely Pussy, O Pussy my love,
What a beautiful Pussy you are.
You are, You are,
What a beautiful Pussy you are!

Pussy said to the Owl, 'You elegant fowl,
How charmingly sweet you sing!
O let us be married, too long we have tarried;
But what shall we do for a ring?'

They sailed away, for a year and a day,
To the land where the Bong-tree grows,
And there in a wood a Piggy-wig stood
With a ring at the end of his nose,
His nose, His nose,
With a ring at the end of his nose.

'Dear Pig, are you willing to sell for one shilling
Your ring?' Said the Piggy, "I will'.
So they took it away, and were married next day
By the Turkey who lives on the hill.
They dined on mince, and slices of quince,
Which they ate with a runcible spoon.
And hand in hand, on the edge of the sand,
They danced by the light of the moon,
The moon, The moon,
They danced by the light of the moon.

Edward Lear (1871)

1
AFTER THE HONEYMOON

Fasten with all your might on the inestimable treasure of your liking for each other and your understanding of each other — build your life on its secure foundations, and let everything you do and think be a part of it . . . times come when one would give anything in the world for a reason like that for living on.

Letter from Edith Wharton to her niece Beatrix Jones (Trix) on her wedding day, in 1913, a year after Wharton's divorce.

In Cinderella's story 'we got married and lived happily ever after' is the end of the adventure. But in real life, of course, it's just the beginning. And 'real life' is the key here. It can bring us down to earth with a bump, and it can happen sooner than we expect. Even when couples have already been living together for some time, they tend to have heightened expectations of married life. Other aspects of family life may have become fraught and filled us with cynicism, but the idea of marriage, or rather the act of 'getting married', as the longed-for climax to falling in love, is still strong.

The rituals that go with a wedding reinforce the dream, and we perform them with as much commitment and enthusiasm as ever. At the stag night and hen party the bride and groom say farewell to their carefree, single lives. The importance of the wedding ceremony as a rite of passage is emphasised by the bride's beautiful dress and unaccustomed glamorous hairstyle; the groom's suit and tie and close shave; the mother's tears, the father's speech; the confetti, the mind-blowing cost of the bubbly and chocolate fountain; and, above all, the solemn vows they make. It is, they say, to console themselves for the crippling financial outlay, a once-in-a-lifetime occasion. And then... whoosh, off on honeymoon, and whoosh, you are home again, ready to embark on the rest of your lives.

Imagine the scene... a young couple return home after a blissful honeymoon in the tropics. At quarter to midnight they pay off the taxi from the airport and lug their bags up to their second-floor flat. Outside the door, he feels in his pocket. It's empty.

'You've got the key,' he says.

She rummages in her handbag. No key.

'I remember,' she says. 'I handed it to you when we locked up.'

'I don't think so. It would be in my pocket. I was wearing this jacket.'

'Well, if you haven't got it, I don't know who has. Certainly not me – I keep my keys zipped up in the inner pocket of my bag. Look: car key, key to the office. Nothing else.'

He turns his jacket pockets out, leaving the linings hanging out. She thinks he looks silly, and giggles.

'If this is your idea of a joke, I don't think much of it.'

'If this is your idea of efficiency, I don't think much of it.'

She empties the handbag on the floor – still no key. They eventually ring her mother, who gets out of bed and comes round with the spare key. Exhausted, the newly-weds fall into bed without unpacking, seething with mutual resentment and barely speaking. The atmosphere is no better the next morning when they leave for work. It's not until the evening, when they finally get round to unpacking, that they find the key, tucked for safety into a pair of socks.

The honeymooners have just had their first 'domestic'. As rows go, it's trivial, and they'll laugh about it in years to come. But, at the moment, it all matters hugely, and they are probably taking themselves a little too seriously.

Our own honeymoon – 47 years ago in a delightful small hotel in Ibiza – was certainly a once-in-a-lifetime holiday, though it could not be described as an unalloyed success. We began it in a broom cupboard. I had booked the 'Napoleonic Suite', a grand name for a spacious bedroom with an almost equally spacious bathroom and balcony. Unfortunately, my handwriting made '14th July' look like '19th'. For the first two nights the only available accommodation was a tiny room with a single bed where the maids kept their buckets and mops. We managed, and the Napoleonic Suite seemed all the more romantic when we finally moved in.

Immediately before he married his wife Emma, the writer and actor Julian Fellowes wrote that: 'I had reached that realisation without which no marriage stands a chance, viz after you have done this thing everything is going to change. Life will hopefully be better, it may of course be worse, but one thing is sure: it will be different.'

Actually being married seemed so crowded with unspoken rules and odd secrets and unfathomable responsibilities that it had no more occurred to her to imagine being married herself than it had to imagine driving a motorcycle or having a job. She had, however, thought about being a bride, which had more to do with being the centre of attention and looking inexplicably, temporarily

Our own honeymoon was certainly a once-in-a-lifetime holiday, though it could not be described as an unalloyed success.

*beautiful than it did withsharing a double bed
with someone with hairy legs and a drawer full of
boxer shorts.*

Object Lessons, Anna Quindlen (1991)

Marriage does indeed change domestic life in many subtle ways. The transition from 'mine' and 'his' to 'ours' can be tricky, whether it's a jar of Marmite or a difficult friend. When a couple spends more time at home together, sharing a small living space can lead to territorial disputes, needing diplomatic negotiation to resolve them. Such mundane matters as whose books go on which shelves and whether his mother's cracked pie dish can be thrown away become important issues to be argued over at length, although they will seem ridiculously unimportant in retrospect.

A certain competitive house-proudness can also take over newly-weds. More weekend time is spent on trips to Ikea and Homebase than ever seemed possible and individual tastes in wallpaper, cushion covers or lampshades may suddenly seem radically different. Our first row occurred before Rob and I were married when we were choosing household items for our wedding present list. Be warned that the words 'But you can't like those plates, they're hideous' are not endearing to a future spouse.

There is something about actually being married,

knowing that one has tied oneself irrevocably to another person, that highlights problems that one had not ever known were there. Behaviour that was hardly noticed before suddenly becomes a major source of irritation; personal habits, which previously had seemed acceptable, start to fill the observer with disgust – although men and women seem to differ in their views about the seriousness of these. The husband who said, 'I find bodily functions funny and she most certainly doesn't', probably hit the nail on the head.

It's logical to think that, if we are not satisfied with the way our spouse behaves, we should set about changing it. But both men and women should understand that change will only ever be marginal. No one can turn a sow's ear into a silk purse, an untidy, absent-minded boffin into a suit-and-tie executive; or vice versa. Brooding on a partner's defects condemns us to a lifetime of discontent. Better turn our thoughts to a partner's positive aspects, the aspects we fell in love with in the first place.

For if, as very occasionally happens, we succeed in moulding a partner into an ideal, we may end up wishing we had the old, imperfect model back. The plot where a haughty beauty spurns the love of a strong, silent rough diamond is a familiar one in romantic fiction. The rejected suitor goes off to acquire some style and polish, and when he returns as a fashionable fop, the beauty realises that she loved the rough diamond all along.

The key is not to start out in marriage with unrealistic expectations. As one husband in a happy marriage

MARRY THE MAN TODAY

Marry the man today.
Trouble though he may be,
Much as he likes to play
Crazy and wild and free.

Marry the man today
Rather than sigh in sorrow,
Marry the man today
And change his ways tomorrow.

Marry the man today
Give him the girlish laughter
Give him your hand today
And save the fist for after.

Slowly introduce him to the better things
Respectable, conservative and clean.
Readers Digest. Golf! Galoshes. Ovaltine!
But marry the man today
Handle it meek and gently
Marry the man today and train him subsequently.

**Sung by Adelaide and Sarah
in *Guys and Dolls* (1950)**

told me, 'Two intelligent, sane people from roughly the same background should be able to make it work. It's too much idealism that can cause doubt and misery.' It's easy to fall into the trap of assuming that the delicious state of heightened emotion, of being 'in love', will last for ever: but would Romeo and Juliet or Cathy and Heathcliff have lived happily ever after? And can we be sure the Darcys' marriage wasn't sabotaged by in-law trouble?

Fortunately, there are plenty of couples celebrating their silver and golden weddings, to prove it can be done. Their advice can be summed up in three recommendations: understand from the start that it won't always be easy; listen to the advice of those who have come through the bad times and enjoyed the good times; and keep your sense of humour.

Perhaps the government of Dubai should be allowed to have the last word here. Dubai's political leaders may not seem to be the most obvious source of marital advice but they have clearly understood the need for mutual realism and compromise. They recently teamed up with welfare agencies and, rather bizarrely, the police, to publish a marriage guidance pamphlet, in the hope of reducing a divorce rate approaching 50 per cent. Appealingly packaged to look like a wedding invitation, the pamphlet offers all sorts of eminently sensible tips. It's not very PC, but there's lots here that you can't argue with...

Dear Husband

Your woman is a different biological human being.
Don't expect her to behave the way you do.

Don't ignore her complaints.
She expects emotional support.

A woman doesn't like a miser, so don't be stingy.

Don't begrudge her visits to her parents.

Don't forget to flirt with her and satisfy her desire.

No verbal assaults.

Don't expect her to solve problems in a reasonable
way. She is too passionate to solve them logically.

Don't interfere in how she runs the house.
Let her feel the queen of her nest.

Try to satisfy her femininity by admiring her
clothes,make-up, cooking.

Take into consideration her mood swings.

A woman is a social being. Don't try to restrict her
freedom in social relations.

A husband committing adultery is the harshest issue
to a woman, so don't even think about doing it.

Dear Wife

Don't compare yourself to him.
He is different.

Don't provoke the cruel nature in your man.
When he is nervous, he can lose his patience
instantly.

Don't expect him to do what you like doing, for he
does not think the same way you do.

A man doesn't like a talkative woman.
Don't nag because it will only confuse him.

Don't wait for him to say sorry because he doesn't
like to apologise. If he wants to express regret,
he will do it indirectly.

Don't tell him something he doesn't like
because doing this would hurt his feelings and
ruin his mood.

Don't nag him all the time because he likes
to be free as a bird.

Don't be a demanding wife because he
likes a contented woman.

A man's generosity lies in his reactions so
don't wait for his initiative.

MARRIAGE GUIDANCE PAMPHLET, DUBAI

YES, I'LL MARRY YOU

Yes, I'll marry you, my dear,
And here's the reason why;
So I can push you out of bed
When the baby starts to cry,
And if we hear a knocking
And it's creepy and it's late,
I hand you the torch you see,
And you investigate.

Yes, I'll marry you, my dear,
You may not apprehend it,
But when the tumble-drier goes
It's you that has to mend it,
You have to face the neighbour
Should our Labrador attack him,
And if a drunkard fondles me
It's you that has to whack him.

Yes, I'll marry you,
You're virile and you're lean,
My house is like a pigsty
You can help to keep it clean.
And that sexy little dinner
Which you served by candlelight,
As I just do chipolatas,
You can cook it every night!

It's you who has to work the drill
And put up curtain track,
And when I've got the PMT it's you who gets the flak.
I do see great advantages,
But none of them for you,
And so before you see the light, I do, I do, I do!

Pam Ayres (1997)

2
HOME SWEET HOME

The Domestic Front Line

When two people move in together, they usually pool
their resources and their chaos, and nothing much changes. They may have the usual arguments about who didn't
clean the bath, whose turn it is to wash up, and who forgot
to buy loo roll, but somehow the housework gets done,
even if not very thoroughly. It's pretty much like any other
flat-sharing arrangement, except that they sleep together.

When they decide to get married, however, or start a
family, their status subtly changes. Suddenly it's no longer
acceptable to let the dirty dishes pile up in the sink until
there are no plates to eat from, or allow the tide mark on
the bath to thicken indefinitely. It's time to recognise that
grown-up couples *do* wash clothes, make beds, dust and
clean on a regular basis.

With their rational caps on, both sexes seem to agree
on this:

Actions speak louder than words. Being unselfish on a daily basis in ways that give pleasure can make you happy as well as your partner, cooking what he likes, watching his favourite TV programme even if it bores you, putting the rubbish out.

♥

When she nags or complains, instead of resenting it, act to put it right before you forget again — replace the light bulb, mend the trouser pocket. But do it, not in the expectation of acknowledgement but for your own satisfaction in a job completed.

♥

Don't expect to be praised for unloading the dishwasher occasionally unless you regularly mete out thanks for the washed and ironed shirts which appear as if by magic in your wardrobe.

If your beloved drops cigarette butts in a half-empty coffee mug, however, or eats with her mouth open, or belches at the table, or habitually leaves socks and pants on the bathroom floor, 'Till death us do part' may sometimes seem like a life sentence. Cumulatively, such trivial annoyances form the tip of a mighty iceberg — indeed, if any of these dismaying habits seem familiar, act now. Resentment is harmful when bottled up, so let it out into the open. 'Better an empty house than a bad tenant,' as my father was fond of saying, in a similar context. And at least two of the habits listed above are things which neither men nor women would normally do if anyone else was present, so to do them when one's spouse is in the room is to treat that person like a piece of furniture: not acceptable.

Back in the early 19th century, William Cobbett, a model husband if ever there was one, seems to have been far in advance of his time.

———————

When her neighbours [in Philadelphia] used to ask my wife whether all English husbands were like hers, she boldly answered in the affirmative. I had business to occupy the whole of my time, Sundays and weekdays, except sleeping hours; but I used to make time to assist her in the taking care of her baby, and in all sorts of things: get up, light her fire, boil her tea-kettle, carry her up warm water in cold weather, take the child while she dressed herself and got the breakfast ready, then breakfast, get her in water and wood for the day, then dress myself neatly, and sally forth to my business. The moment that was over I used to hasten back to her again and I no more thought of spending a moment away from her, unless business compelled me, than I thought of quitting the country and going to sea.

Advice to Young Men and (Incidentally) to Young Women, William Cobbett (1829)

———————

Some 150 years after Cobbett, the only domestic duties I remember my father performing were stoking the boiler, sharpening the knives, carving the Sunday roast and sometimes helping wash up. But he did polish our shoes until we could see our faces in them. My mother liked it that way. The sight of a man with a duster made her (and her friends) uneasy. They considered housework unmanly: in their view, the breadwinner should be waited on when he came home from work.

Most people no longer automatically presume that a woman's place is in the home, but there are still a few men around who grow up with an image of the perfect wife as one who dusts and polishes. They hope for a wife who, like their mothers and grandmothers and George Washington's wife, Martha, will be 'steady as a clock, busy as a bee and cheerful as a cricket'. It doesn't occur to such a man to perform the simplest household task for himself; to him a tidy, cared-for house is a reassuring sign that he is cared for by a loving woman.

Such men must be introduced to housework gradually, and with tact.

To others, domestic skills come naturally. Sometimes too naturally. After 50 years of marriage, one wife admits: 'I nearly didn't marry him at all. I was watching him pack a suitcase one day. He had little boxes for this and little envelopes for that. Far too pernickety. I thought, will I be able to stand living with this person? We're too different. Now, looking back, it's extraordinary how much importance I attached to trivial incidents. But I have since found that although he's fussy about minor points that don't matter, he's almost rashly adventurous about major issues – a trait I love.'

'Excessive cleanliness is a legacy she inherited from her mother,' says one man. 'I'd rather have a bit of dust lying around the house if it meant she would be more relaxed, but she says she has lowered her standards already and she was brought up to polish the furniture every day and clean the silver every time it's used.'

Another complains: 'She snatches my plate away almost before I've put my fork down. I only have to put the newspaper down by my chair for a second, for her to whisk it away.' Problems can also occur when either person has a different idea of what constitutes clutter. One partner's vitally important paperwork is another's litter, destined to be regularly gathered up and deposited in the recycling bin.

In our house it was my father who was tidy to a fault, and he sometimes found my mother, who had no interest at all in housework, difficult to live with. He always knew if his nail file had been moved an inch away from his comb when his dressing table was dusted.

More easy-going creatures, brought up in homes where bohemian clutter was the style, will find a busy bee hard to live with, and the busy bee will see the messy one as a slob. But it can still work. It just needs a little give and take, and understanding of each other's foibles.

Homo Domesticus?

Jan ye 4. This morn we did wake up to see every place covered with snow, it falling right heartily in the night, and work on the land be at the stand still, nought bein done but to feed the stock. So today we plagued mightilie with John in the house, bringin this and that to do and mend, till my clean kitchen be verrie sluty with the snow he do bring in; and me so wroth there at, I do say to get out to the back-house with his messy jobbes, and so he goes off there-to, saying never was a man so plagued with a parcel of women, they being the verrie divvel round a man. At which we laffing, he do stamp out, banging the door mightilie.

The Diary of a Farmer's Wife, 1796-97, Anne Hughes

The frustrations to which Anne Hughes gave voice in the 18th century are still felt by many modern wives. But, although women complain a great deal, it seems they are often simply relieving their feelings by going through a time-honoured ritual, with no expectation that anything will change. It's as if they have accepted that there are incurable male traits that have to be lived with — it's just a question of how. Men, when asked about housework, have far fewer complaints. Does this mean they are more tolerant than women, or do they have fewer grounds for complaint, or are they merely less observant?

For worse, she says

In our house at any one time there's a trail of his clutter from the kitchen through the lobby, bedroom, drawing room, study, bathroom, studio — clothes, shoes, garden tools, newspapers, magazines, books, papers, paintings — seven pairs of spectacles in the kitchen as I write, five combs on the bedroom floor — no surface in any room is mess-free, every other annoyance pales into oblivion.

♥

He thinks cleaning the house is a spectator sport, and stands with a mug of coffee in his hand watching me vacuum, wipe the worktops and clean the bath, then says, 'You missed a bit here.'

♥

He always walks straight through the house from the garden with muddy shoes, plod, plod, plod, great black yeti footprints on the rug, the floorboards, and finally the utility room floor. Does he think I'm going to follow him round with a dustpan and brush and a mop?

♥

After years of doing all the thinking re children's socks / Cheerios / nits / logistics, I recently cracked. In a blind rage I dragged all his clothes — jeans, shirts, socks, underpants, the lot — out of cupboards and drawers, and tipped them all into the playpen in the kitchen.

♥

Capability is sexy and life affirming. It turns me off when he is helpless and incompetent.

♥

He offers to help but every day, every week, I have to tell him what needs doing. I would love it if he would just think for himself, see what needs doing and bloody well do it.

♥

It takes time to train them… We've been married 13 years and after the third child he seems to have the hang of it.

For worse, he says

It's a traditional division of labour; I work, she looks after the kids, we share chores as much as we can. I do all the handyman stuff.

♥

Being a man I tend not to see dirt or mess and regard washing up as something to be done when you run out of plates — so I've been allocated some 'manly' jobs like putting out the rubbish.

♥

She does the cooking and childcare, I do the washing and ironing and we share the cleaning. Well, perhaps 'share' isn't quite the right word.

♥

I do everything except the washing and ironing.

RULE FOUR: The wife who keeps saying 'Isn't that just like a man?' and the husband who keeps saying, 'Oh, well, you know how women are,' are likely to grow farther and farther apart through the years. These famous generalisations have the effect of reducing an individual to the anonymous status of a mere unit in a mass. The wife who, just in time, comes upon her husband about to fry an egg in a dry skillet should not classify him with all other males but should give him the accolade of a special distinction. She might say, for example, 'George, no other man in the world would try to do a thing like that.' Similarly, a husband watching his wife labouring to start the car without turning on the ignition should not say to the gardener or a passerby, 'Oh, well, you know', etc. Instead, he should remark to his wife, 'I've seen a lot of women in my life, Nelie, but I've never seen one who could touch you.'

One wife, reading Rule Four over my shoulder, exclaimed, 'Isn't that just like a man?' This brings us right back where we started. Oh, well, you know how women are!

My Own Ten Rules for a Happy Marriage, James Thurber (1953)

In some partnerships, traditional roles are reversed. There are wives like me, who wield the Black and Decker, unblock the drains and change the plugs. My husband tells our friends that I enjoy lying on my stomach in the back yard with my arm down the sewage outlet pipe. Not so. I do it because if I don't, nobody else will. It's true there's a certain satisfaction about getting a drain to flow again freely, but in spite of much encouragement and helpful suggestions from the sidelines, I could never say getting that particular job done gave me much pleasure.

If arguments about housework keep recurring, it's possible housework has become a metaphor for deeper-seated feelings about 'pulling weight' in other respects, one partner having an unconscious conviction that the other is selfish or even lacking in love. For some couples it helps to work out a rota of chores and pin it up on the fridge alongside the children's star charts. Not that I am suggesting for a minute that grown-ups award each other stars for effort, but there is some satisfaction to be had from mentally ticking off achievements.

In the end, it makes sense for each person to do what they're good at and enjoy doing (as much as domestic chores can be enjoyable). There are happy households where the man cooks, washes, irons and looks after the children, and the couple shares the cleaning. Others prefer their parents' traditional routine with the homebody doing the housework and the wage slave taking out the rubbish and tackling DIY, decorating and repairs.

One wife explains, 'An amicable division of labour has

evolved naturally: we each play to our strengths – he's a good cook so he makes the meals. He's rubbish at cleaning and tidying so I do that. He's a morning person and I'm not, so he gets the children up.'

The kitchen, where I am usually, is too small, and it shrinks on the weekends when Bert wants to use it as a workshop. I'm not house proud but as soon as I've done the floor over, he comes in with his muddy feet and wants to bring the pieces of his car in. Naturally, I'm not keen. But he has a go at me saying that you see adverts on the television showing men walking into women's kitchens and making a mess of them and that they have got these marvellous things that clean the floor with no trouble.

The English Marriage, Drusilla Beyfus (1968)

In my view, the first necessity of a harmonious domestic relationship is to come down to a tidy kitchen every morning. We are particularly vulnerable first thing, as we scramble to get the family up, dressed, fed and out of the house to school or work. It's all too horribly familiar but never gets easier. Nothing gets the day off to a worse start than a sink full of dirty pans with grease congealing on them, and a worktop smeared with last night's ketchup. The partner who does the dishes and wipes the surfaces last thing before bed, should help themselves to a halo and may be forgiven for minor early-morning misdemeanours, such as drinking juice straight out of the carton, and not screwing the jam lid back properly.

Kitchen Confidential

The jelly that wouldn't jell

Meg, newly married and house-proud, has decided to stock her new larder with pots of currant jelly. She spent a long day 'picking, boiling, straining, and fussing over her jelly. She did her best... she re-boiled, re-sugared, and re-strained, but that dreadful stuff wouldn't "jell"... At five o'clock she sat down in her topsy-turvy kitchen, wrung her bedaubed hands, lifted up her voice and wept...'
And that was the moment her husband John chose to come home, accompanied by an unannounced dinner guest.

'In the kitchen reigned confusion and despair; one edition of jelly was trickled from pot to pot, another lay upon the floor, and a third was burning gaily on the stove... while Meg, with her apron over her head, sat sobbing dismally.

'My dearest girl, what is the matter?' cried John...

'Oh, John, I am so tired, and hot, and cross, and worried! I've been at it till I'm worn out. Do come and help me, or I shall die…'

'What worries you, dear? Has anything dreadful happened?'…

'Yes,' sobbed Meg despairingly… 'The — the jelly won't jell, and I don't know what to do!'

John Brooke laughed then as he never dared to laugh afterward…

'Is that all? Fling it out of the window, and don't bother any more about it. I'll buy you quarts if you want it; but, for heaven's sake, don't have hysterics, for I've brought Jack Scott home to dinner.'

Adapted from *Good Wives*, Louisa M Alcott (1869)

———————— ❧ ————————

Once upon a time, as all readers of women's magazines knew, at 6.30 pm every evening the wife was waiting in the hall in a pretty pinny, lipstick freshly applied and hair becomingly arranged, with the table already laid and a delicious dish simmering in the oven.

Not any more, thank God. Today equality is nowhere more clearly displayed than in the kitchen. Meals are just as likely to be prepared and cooked by the man of the house as by his partner and this applies whether she is a stay-at-home mother or the managing director of a multinational company.

If one partner is a better cook than the other, it makes sense for that person to be head chef. Whichever one it is may appreciate help prepping the vegetables, grating the cheese, chopping the herbs and whisking the egg whites, and the less skilled cook might volunteer for these menial tasks. It goes without saying, however, that the glamorous and macho role of head chef does not automatically confer the right to treat the other partner as kitchen skivvy.

'In the kitchen,' the wife of a surgeon complains, 'he speaks to me as if I were a nurse in an operating theatre.' 'She barks orders like a female Gordon Ramsay,' says a husband. Professional chefs who demonstrate a master—slave relationship with their underlings set a bad example, which, if followed, can seriously disrupt domestic harmony.

For better, he says

She cooks delicious meals — every day!

♥

When I cook she washes up my dirty (usually burnt, actually) pots and pans.

♥

At weekends we have terrific cooking sessions, sometimes just ourselves and sometimes with friends. We start with a trip to the farmers' market and end up with a delicious lunch at about 3 o'clock.

♥

For better, she says

He's perfect. He's a whiz in the kitchen.

♥

When we get back from shopping he always unpacks everything and puts it all away while I make a cup of tea. He brings home surprises, like fresh asparagus and other delicacies.

♥

I'm pig-ignorant about wine, but he is a bit of a buff. He thinks I don't appreciate the good wine he buys but I do.

For worse, he says

She leaves minute quantities of leftovers festering in the fridge and half the stuff in the store cupboard is past its sell-by date. If I didn't throw it out it would be there till doomsday.

♥

She fills the kettle to the very top to make just one cup of tea.

♥

She loads the dishwasher as if it were a washing machine — everything chucked in in a heap. I'm always having to redo it.

♥

She puts all the wrong things in the compost bucket so I find myself picking through bits of old peel and coffee grains and broken eggshell to get them out. It's horrible.

♥

For worse, she says

He puts empty cartons back in the fridge.

♥

He never puts lids back on, and puts the mustard back in the fridge with the spoon still in it.

♥

He always leaves the milk out of the fridge so of course it goes off.

♥

He never empties the teapot or cafetiere.

♥

He puts teabags in the sink rather than the bin.

♥

He never shuts the cupboards, not even after I got a black eye walking into an open door.

♥

When he cooks, he takes all the saucepans out of the cupboard to choose the right one for the job, and leaves them out on the worktop for me to put away. Sometimes he then proceeds to use all the saucepans, burns half of them and leaves them for me to wash up.

In a perfect world, preparing food for one's family is a daily act of love; and it deserves appreciation: when questioned, the partners of truly exceptional cooks certainly put food high on their list of things that keep them together as a couple. But the results are unlikely to be perfect every time, and when the soufflé fails to rise or the meat comes out grey, not pink, a tactful attitude is required. Even quite gentle criticism can seem like rejection, not just of the burnt offering but of the cook as well. The critic who stands idly by and throws in occasional comments like 'Aren't you going to use more garlic?'; 'Is that all the broccoli you bought?' and 'You know, I hate to criticise, but I find you never add enough herbs' is asking for trouble. As was the husband I heard of recently who insulted his spouse by retreating to the kitchen after supper to make a triple-decker sandwich.

In the early stages of marriage, failure to take kitchen setbacks seriously enough can seem as great a crime as criticism of trivial faults. Even the least picky eaters have their likes and dislikes, and it's as well to make them known from the start. When we were first married, I made a point of cooking rice pudding at least once a month. A misunderstood remark of my mother-in-law's gave me the impression that, unlike Mary Jane in A. A. Milne's poem, Rob liked 'lovely Rice Pudding for dinner again'. And again and again. It took him several years to break the news to me that this was not so, which just shows how lovely and forbearing he is.

Come Dine with Me

It hardly needs saying that it's good for a relationship if, in the evening, partners sit down to eat together, rather than slump side by side in front of the television with their plates on their laps. This meal, with the children, let's hope, asleep in bed, can be the quiet centre of a couple's day, their one chance to pay attention to each other, talk and make plans for the future. As children grow older and bedtimes get later, the evening meal changes in character, becoming a noisy family event, but still the hub of home life. We all know this is the civilised way to live, although those of us who preach it don't always manage to practise it. But just a few times each week is better than none at all.

Among the couples I talked to, perhaps surprisingly, great importance was attached to the vexed issue of table manners. One husband complained that his wife clears the table before he has finished eating, another that his partner eats jam off a knife, straight from the jar, another that his spouse has a 'revolting habit of picking up crumbs from the table on a damp finger and eating them – I don't think she even knows she is doing it'. Men are accused of eating with their mouths open, licking their knives or plates, or dousing everything with ketchup. 'When he eats crisps he makes the sound of a horse munching an apple,' says a wife. And one husband actually picks his teeth with rolled-up bits of Sellotape then drops them on the floor (the Sellotape, not the teeth).

All Washed up

Dishwashers are meant to make life easier. The latest

models come with a raft of gizmos. But where is the 'performance solution' to the marital friction lurking between the whirlpool cutlery basket and the 'rackmatic' stacking facility?

One of the mysteries of married life is the way two people can have the same argument again and again and again, like the couples who both insist that their own method of loading the dishwasher is the only sensible one. It seems to be a point of honour not to give way on this. Similarly, while both partners know that toast crumbs and mashed potato will stick to the glasses unless the plates are rinsed before loading, one of them will consistently fail to do so, and the other will feel duty-bound to point this out every single time they load the machine.

As for unloading and putting away... in our family the answer is simple. The person with the strongest views about loading (my husband) always loads. And I unload, because he hates putting away. (Don't all men hate putting away?) 'I can't bear the way he acts helpless to get out of ever doing it,' says one desperate wife. 'He knows exactly where everything goes, but just has to put a Tupperware box in the saucepan drawer, or the Magimix blades in with the foil and binliners, to remind me that I'm better off doing it myself...')

For better, he says

In my first marriage, emptying the dishwasher became

Why use one pan when nineteen will do?

*a crazy bone of contention. We'd go for days in silent
dishwasher mutiny, neither of us able to give in… My
new wife is happy for me to load, and she empties. But
more important than that, she'd never allow me to descend
to such childishness as to fight about it.*

For better, she says

*He loads the dishwasher (he says I do it wrong) and
washes up the pots and pans and wipes all the surfaces
after I've gone to bed. I'm eternally grateful — myself,
I'm just too knackered at the end of the day.*

♥

*He does the dishes even if he only has half an hour
lunch break from work because I don't have time
and seeing dirty dishes everywhere stresses me
out!*

For worse, he says

*She leaves cooking utensils unwashed but the food is
delicious so I forgive her.*

♥

*She always stacks the washing-up on the wrong side of the
sink.*

♥

*She seems to think dishes will wash themselves if she
leaves them to soak and I find them next morning in stale,
greasy water.*

For worse, she says

He fills the sink to the top just to wash one mug or if there's lots of washing-up he puts it all in the sink at once so you can't get your hands in to actually wash anything.

♥

He always, always leaves just a little pile of mayo or mustard on his plate, and when I ask him to scrape it off, he flicks most of it on to the bin lid.

♥

He washes up with cold water, just spreading the grease around on the surfaces of plates and mugs instead of washing it off.

♥

My husband is an absolute stickler about washing-up. Most nights he silently rewashes things I've washed already. I might have left a tiny smear but I find it completely maddening.

♥

He uses 19 pans when one would do. Don't all men?

A frequent wives' moan is that husbands suffer from selective blindness. A wife explains: 'He just can't see what needs doing and will happily leave a trail of dirty teacups in the bedroom behind him as he goes downstairs in the morning, apparently convinced that someone more attentive is going to be following behind him.'

I wonder if it occurs to the complaining wives that

selective blindness is due to lack of training? It seems odd
that, after three years of marriage, one husband still 'has
to be shown where the kettle is'.

If many men appear to lack a fundamental talent for
domesticity, though, there are plenty of women who
could be accused of the same, women who litter newspapers all over the kitchen table, leave sticky rings after
jam pots, walk mud through the house or leave dog biscuits scattered over the worktop. And there's a good deal
of sexism here. Inveterately untidy women tend to be por-
trayed as scatty and eccentric, whereas a man who readily
dons rubber gloves to wash up is scorned as an unsexy
wimp.

*Alfred and I are happy, as happy as married
people can be. We are in love, we are intellectu-
ally and physically suited in every possible way, we
rejoice in each other's company. We have no money
troubles and three delightful children. And yet
when I consider my life, day by day, hour by hour,
it seems to be composed of a series of pin-pricks.
Nannies, cooks, the endless drudgery of housekeeping, the nerve-racking noise and boring repetitive conversation of small children (boring in
the sense that it bores into one's very brain), their
absolute incapacity to amuse themselves, their
sudden and terrifying illnesses, Alfred's not infrequent bouts of moodiness, his invariable com-*

plaints at meals about the pudding, the way he will use the toothpaste and will always squeeze the tube in the middle. These are the components of marriage, the wholemeal bread of life, rough, ordinary but sustaining.

The Pursuit of Love, Nancy Mitford (1945)

'It All Goes into the Laundry, but It Never Comes Out in the Wash...'

MAN STRANGLES FIANCÉE AFTER ROW OVER WASHING

He is believed to have strangled her during an argument after she asked him to put a load of washing in the machine. He told police later that he could not operate it. 'She said I could not switch the washing machine on, which I couldn't.'

Daily Telegraph, 8 November 2005

Ever since the invention of the washing machine, marriages have been beset by little laundry miseries: underpants dyed pink, scorched trousers, a new cashmere sweater shrunk to fit a 12-year-old... None of these mishaps, however, causes as much strife as the divorced sock. It's not something that affects women, but mystifyingly a pair of men's socks, during its transition through the wash, seems almost honour-bound to become half a pair, useful only to a one-legged husband. In many households, the lone sock is cause of a daily frisson of irritation. My husband solved the problem by having ten identical pairs of socks, compensating in other sartorial areas for the sacrifice of self-expression on his feet. However, I've recently noticed the odd pair of gaudy socks creeping back into the laundry basket, and I'm afraid it will only be a matter of time before bereavement occurs.

Washing clothes, it seems, is still one of those jobs in the house that women undertake on their own. Those women who have brought up the current generation of men may have taught their sons, as well as daughters, to cook and clean, but somehow they never got round to teaching their boys to look after their clothes. 'His mother did everything for him,' a wife explains. 'He does his fair share of most chores, but I've had to teach him how the washing machine works and how to iron a shirt.'

There are men, punctilious about putting on clean underclothes every day, who hardly realise their discarded clothes need washing. A wife reports, 'He'll happily walk round a pile of his own dirty clothes and not notice them.' Another, furious with her husband after a blazing row, decided to punish him by not washing his clothes. She had to abandon her campaign after two weeks, because he just hadn't cottoned on.

A mother who allows her student son to bring dirty laundry home at weekends may turn into a mother-in-law who expects her daughter-in-law to iron her husband's shirts. She's asking for trouble, especially if she grabs the ironing board to tackle the job herself. The innocent words 'You have so much to do, why don't I just iron a couple of his shirts for you?' may seem neutral, but to a daughter-in-law they are code for 'You don't look after my son properly'.

What to do? According to Annie, a Croatian woman interviewed recently in the *Sunday Telegraph*, men have no business being anywhere near an ironing board: 'I remember finding my first British boyfriend, who was a real rugby-playing type, ironing. I was totally shocked,' she recalls. 'I offered to do it for him, but he got quite huffy and said he ironed better than his mother... In Croatia men sit on the sofa with a beer and women run around and look after the house. You may think me a peasant, but I think it's my job to cook and do laundry, while the man fixes the car.'

Most British women will baulk at Annie's idea of a fair division of labour but, when it comes to ironing, as we all know from experience, it's quicker to do it ourselves. By the time we've shown him how to put the ironing board up, plug in the iron, turn the dial to the right temperature and operate the spray to damp the shirt, we could have worked our way through half a clean linen basket.

Parlour Games

RULE SIX: A husband should try to remember where things are around the house so that he does not have to wait for his wife to get home from the hairdresser's before he can put his hands on what he wants. Among the things a husband is usually unable to locate are the iodine, the aspirin, the nail file, the French vermouth, his cuff links, studs, black silk socks and evening shirts, the snapshots taken at Nantucket last summer, his favourite record of 'Kentucky Babe', the borrowed copy of My Cousin Rachel, the garage key, his own towel, the last bill from Brooks Bros, his pipe cleaners, the poker chips, crackers, cheese, the whetstone, his new raincoat, and the screens for the upstairs windows. I don't really know the solution to this problem, but one should be found. Perhaps every wife should draw for her husband a detailed map of the house, showing clearly the location of everything he might need. Trouble is, I suppose, he would lay the map down somewhere and not be able to find it until his wife got home.

My Own Ten Rules for a Happy Marriage, James Thurber (1953)

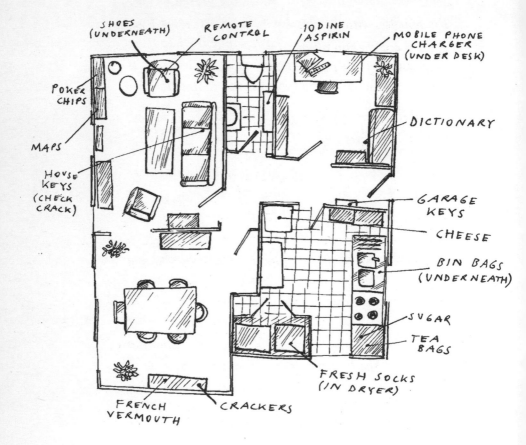

*'Every wife should draw for her husband a
detailed map of the house, showing clearly the
location of everything he might need...'*

For better, he says

I make a terrible mess with bits of the newspaper all over the place but she never complains.

♥

I'm hopeless with my possessions — have been since I was a child — but she can always find my diary, pen, specs, book and anything else I've mislaid.

♥

She always gets out of my favourite chair when I come in, although it's hers too.

For better, she says

In the evening he pours me a perfect vodka and tonic or gets a lovely bottle of wine and we sit down to share it; it's top of my list every day, so greatly appreciated.

♥

He loves a good fire and, to my joy, undertakes every aspect of it: brings in the logs, lights the fire, tends it, and never lets it go out. If he has to go away for a few days he always makes sure the log basket is filled and the fire laid in the grate ready to be lit, as I'm hopeless at making fires.

♥

He's good about picking up after the children — I'm too knackered to pick up all their toys and sweep up their crumbs at the end of the day.

♥

For worse, he says

She puts flowers in inconvenient places, so I knock them over, causing mayhem.

♥

She complains about the dogs: their hairs everywhere, their slobber, their farting and their flailing tails, but they're my pride and joy!

♥

She just comes into the room where I am and turns the music up or changes it and, even more annoying, reduces the level of the lighting. Then leaves the room. And then I have to change it all back. After 35 years she must know I hate it.

♥

She has no concentration so we can't read in the same room — even if all I'm doing is turning the pages of a newspaper.

For worse, she says

He likes the main light on, I like the lamps. We have argued about this for 15 years.

♥

He chucks biscuit wrappers behind the sofa when there's a perfectly good bin.

♥

If he starts a sentence, 'I can't find...' I've learned not to stop what I'm doing and look for it. It's usually right in front of his nose and he just asks out of sheer habit. As soon as I get up to look for whatever it is, he will say, 'Oh here it is.'

♥

He doesn't give telephone messages — he writes them down on the newspaper or magazine he's reading at the time, but doesn't remember to deliver them.

♥

He always leaves the door open when he goes from one room to another: 'born in a tent', as my grandmother used to say. We eventually solved the problem by taking the doors between the hall, the kitchen and the sitting room off their hinges and storing them in the garage, so now we have open-plan living. I'm thinking of applying the same remedy to the wardrobe doors that he leaves gaping open in our bedroom.

'What's on the Box?'

Without a doubt the key flashpoint in the living room is the TV. In this area, men, it seems, have the upper hand, getting away with channel-hopping, watching sport and 'endless reruns of *Top Gear*'.

'My husband is forever flicking between racing and rugby, the Bloomberg Channel, online poker, anything with battle scenes, and just boring stuff,' laments one wife. 'In eight years,' another says wistfully, 'I've never seen an ad on TV. As soon as a programme has a break he switches to another channel.' Men automatically take possession of the remote control, to the point where 'if I'm watching and he comes in, he holds his hand out for it'. Perhaps control of the TV zapper symbolises other forms of control. Men certainly seem to have an uncanny attachment to it. No matter how deeply asleep a man is, no sooner does a stealthy hand attempt gently to remove it from his grasp, than he wakes with a start and clutches it tighter.

Men justify this behaviour on the grounds that their wives have no discernment about what is worth watching and what not. Most men simply can't understand why women 'won't watch anything with violence/blood'. As for the female passion for soap operas, the only escape is the pub. Then there is the annoying sort of wife who won't settle to watch a programme, but comes in halfway through and asks for an explanation of the plot, thereby causing her partner to miss the next bit.

For better, she says
He lets me watch Desperate Housewives, *even though he hates it. Most of my friends have to save this up for solitary late-night sessions alone.*

For worse, she says
He switches channels then says, 'You weren't watching that, were you?'

♥

[60]

I'm forever going into an empty room to find the TV talking to itself; it drives me up the wall.

♥

He goes to sleep in front of the TV, even though I've told him to go to bed because I can see he's about to fall asleep. There he sits snoring. It's impossible to rouse him, but when he wakes up aching on the sofa at 3am he complains as if it's my fault.

♥

My husband is a TV addict. He watches it all the time and I can't help but find it insulting. After spending all day with an 18-week-old baby, it would be nice to have some adult conversation.

The average UK household boasts 4.5 TV sets (yes, really, and if you live in Ballymacbrennan, Northern Ireland, it's 6.2), so in theory both partners should be able to watch their programme of choice. The fact that they complain about each other's preferred viewing is encouraging evidence that they would rather spend the evening together, with one of them bored, than separately, with both of them entertained. This challenges the theory that too much time spent in close proximity is bad for a marriage, an idea developed by Rebecca West. She wrote: 'The English Victorian middle class practically never got divorced... look at the villas they lived in... they had plenty of room to get away from each other… But a husband and wife living in a three-roomed apartment or a bungalow cannot move more than a few yards from the scene of their disagreements, and have no such chance to break away and forget and start again.'

In some cases, television may help keep couples happy as it gives them somewhere to escape to in their minds, away from their mutual grievances. But in the past 15 years another threat to marital communication has developed. Any spare time at home not spent in front of the TV is likely these days to be spent in front of a computer.

Obviously, for people who have few opportunities to go out, because they have children or old people to care for, the internet and television are lifelines, but as far as domestic bliss is concerned, computers are a mixed blessing. With so much time taken up checking emails, uploading photographs, surfing websites and ordering groceries online, there is precious little time left for family life.

And as for mobile phones… I can imagine a scene where two people sit side by side on a sofa, in front of a TV screen. Both have laptop computers on the coffee table, but they are not looking at the TV or the computer screen. Their heads are bent low, one hand in a packet of crisps, the other busy on the keypad of a mobile phone. They are conversing with each other – by text message.

It doesn't have to be like that. Enthusiasts always manage to find time for home-based amusements such as listening to music, playing games, reading, making things or mending a bike. If we hear ourselves saying, 'I'd love to do that, if only I had the time,' we're probably deceiving ourselves. The only things depriving us of time are the TV set and computer. Mr and Mrs Smugly-Perfect's answer is to plan a TV-free night once a week for something they always wanted to do, if only they had the time. It may be teaching each other to play bridge, it could be mastering salsa, or just playing Scrabble. Almost any occupation beats sitting in front of the TV, moaning because, on umpteen channels, there's nothing you both want to watch.

'A Jug of Wine, and Thou...'

A shared bottle of wine at the end of the day is rated highly among the 'for better' aspects of marriage; however, too much booze can have a bad effect on the relationship as well as on the liver. This is not the place to write about extreme cases but even a moderate amount doesn't always bring the desired benefits, and a weekly alcohol-free day (much in the same spirit as a weekly 24-hour freeze on TV) can be good for self-esteem as well as health.

Rosie Millard, writing in *The Times* recently, described very frankly the effect on her marriage of a routine of drinking wine every night, and the improvement to their lives when she and her husband gave it up. 'Our old routine would go thus: get home, play with our four children (aged between one and eight), put them to bed, have supper and a bottle of wine, have a row. Years of sleep deprivation and too much red wine is not a recipe for marital harmony.'

A glass or two of wine a day is said to be good for us, especially as we get older. But when the 'glass or two' becomes a glass or three or four or five (might as well finish the bottle), and when the thought 'God, I need a drink' comes into our head regular as clockwork at the same time towards the end of each gruelling day, alarm bells should be ringing.

Besides increasing the likelihood of a row, alcohol robs us of willpower. After the second glass the decision to pick up the phone to call a lonely friend or relation slowly ebbs away and we decide that our hair can go without washing for another day. We certainly can't be bothered to get out the ironing board or turn up a droopy hem or write a letter. These are admittedly trivial tasks; but when they're repeatedly left undone, things begin to fall apart.

For years I've been thinking about drinking only at weekends, knowing that, if we stuck to it, we'd get more done about the house, be nicer to each other, have more cash in our pockets and lose a few pounds in weight. All so much easier said than done!

Out with the Bathwater. . .

Here's a glimpse of Mrs Perfect's bathroom: the bath and washbasin are spotless, taps gleaming. Large, fluffy towels hang neatly folded on heated rails. The toothpaste has its cap on and has been squeezed from the bottom. Pills, razors, contact lenses, deodorant, hair-removing cream and other unglamorous necessities are stowed away in the cabinet above the washbasin. When you open it, nothing falls out. The only lotions and potions on display come with matching scented candles. In Mr and Mrs P's world, the bathroom is more than just a place to wash. It is a sanctuary, a haven of peace and privacy.

In real life, of course, particularly for couples with a very hectic family life, the bathroom is more often a potential battleground, the room you fight to get into and then hang on to for dear life. Forget that fantasy of a long relaxing bathe at the end of the day: the scented water, the rejuvenating facemask, the chance finally to have a good read of that new novel… No sooner have you settled into that delicious hot water than it will be: 'Mu-um, how long you going to be in there? I'm *desperate!*'

But, if we can't always enjoy quality time in the bathroom, we can at least try to maintain some kind of order there. For even minor breaches of bathroom etiquette, repeated too often, can cause marital friction.

A husband complains that 'her hair blocks the plughole'. Another accuses his wife of 'leaving toenails lying around'. We all know that men leave the floor, the towels and even the loo roll soaking wet, and take a clean towel out of the cupboard every time they have a bath. Poor darlings, they can't help it.

One 'leaves his razor in the tooth-mug, so I cut my finger when I reach for the toothbrush'. In fact, shaving misdemeanours in general seem to be a flashpoint – whether it's his chin or her legs – and are probably best avoided. 'Borrowing' a partner's razor to shave your legs may not be valid evidence in the divorce court, but it is definitely not on!

For better, he says

We have separate bathrooms – it's vital!

♥

She cleans the bath, which I appreciate more than I can say – it's a hateful job.

For better, she says

We always share a bath on Sunday mornings and he always takes the tap end.

♥

He brings me a drink in the bath – bliss.

♥

He always leaves the seat down, to my mind a priceless quality among men.

♥

He hangs up his towels neatly on the rail to dry, which is more than I can say for myself.

For worse, he says
She never remembers to replace the toilet roll, and I'm always caught short.

♥

She hides my shaving and tooth-cleaning equipment.

♥

She leaves the top off the toothpaste and squeezes the toothpaste from the top.

♥

She's a bit strong on the bath salts and likes the water too hot, so after we've shared a bath I look like a lobster and smell like a brothel.

For worse, she says
He leaves wet towels all scrunched up so they don't dry and start smelling.

♥

He thinks the fairies live at our house and magic his dirty clothes off the floor and into the washing basket.

♥

He never ever cleans the loo and that, surely, is a man's job!

♥

*Even minor breaches of bathroom etiquette,
repeated too often, can cause marital friction.*

I WANNA BE YOURS

I wanna be your vacuum cleaner
breathing in your dust
I wanna be your Ford Cortina
I will never rust
If you like your coffee hot
let me be your coffee pot
You call the shots
I wanna be yours

I wanna be your raincoat for those frequent rainy days
I wanna be your dreamboat
when you want to sail away
Let me be your teddy bear
take me with you anywhere
I don't care
I wanna be yours

I wanna be your electric meter
I will not run out
I wanna be the electric heater
you'll get cold without
I wanna be your setting lotion
hold your hair in deep devotion
Deep as the deep Atlantic ocean
that's how deep is my devotion

John Cooper Clarke (1982)

Most Glorious Night!

Marriage is an alliance entered into by a man who can't sleep with the window shut, and a woman who can't sleep with the window open.
George Bernard Shaw (1856-1950)

A man marries to have a home but also because he doesn't want to be bothered with sex and all that sort of thing.
W Somerset Maugham (1874-1965)

I'm not going to discuss the most obvious activity that takes place in the bedroom but it's worth mentioning that there is no such thing as a 'normal' sex life, and that the importance attached to sex in a marriage varies enormously from one couple to another. Some make love three or four times a week, others three or four times a year, and in each case they may regard their marriage as happy. Having exchanged, in Mrs Patrick Campbell's famous words, 'the hurly-burly of the chaise-longue for the deep, deep peace of the double bed', some couples, especially after a few decades together, rate cuddles and considerateness higher than sex.

As in the kitchen, living room and bathroom, it is the seemingly trivial pleasures or annoyances in the bedroom that, when added up, contribute to or detract from marital contentment.

RULE TEN: A wife's dressing table should be inviolable. It is the one place in the house a husband should get away from and stay away from. And yet, the average husband is drawn to it as by a magnet, especially when he is carrying something wet, oily, greasy or stocky such as a universal joint, a hub cap, or the blades of a lawn mower. His excuse for bringing these alien objects into his wife's bedroom in the first place is that he is looking for 'an old rag' with which to wipe them off. There are no old rags in a lady's boudoir, but husbands never seem to learn this. They search hampers, closets, and bureau drawers, expecting to find a suitable piece of cloth, but first they set the greasy object on the dressing table. The aggrieved wife may be tempted, following this kind of vandalism, to lock her bedroom door and kick her husband out for good. I suggest, however, a less stringent punishment. Put a turtle in his bed. The wife who is afraid to pick up a turtle should ask Junior to help her. Junior will love it.

My Own Ten Rules for a Happy Marriage, James Thurber (1953)

For better, he says

She warms up my side of the bed in the winter.

♥

She lets me sleep in on Sunday while she goes downstairs to give the kids breakfast.

♥

We never let the sun go down on an argument.

♥

When I stay up late she sleeps with the light on so I can see what I'm doing when I come to bed.

For better, she says

He keeps me warm and safe every night, always kisses me goodnight and cuddles me until I fall asleep.

♥

He's always been a wonderful lover and still is after 40 years.

♥

I'm the untidy one with make-up scattered all over the dressing table and clothes on the floor, but he turns a blind eye and doesn't complain.

♥

He likes the windows and curtains wide open. So do I.

♥

We often go to bed early, watch TV and snuggle up – it's lovely.

♥

He always brings me coffee in the morning.

For worse, he says

She nags me to pick up my clothes off the floor after I've already got into bed.

♥

She always leaves her clothes in a mess on the floor and leaves her shoes so they trip me up when I get out of bed in the dark.

♥

There's a constant battle whether or not to have the window open and how far open; if it's not wide open I am stifled, but if it's open at all she says there's a howling draught.

♥

She tidies my bits and pieces away in the wrong drawers so I can't find them.

♥

She takes 90% of the clothes storage space and 90 per cent of the duvet.

For worse, she says

He has this special trick which involves taking off trousers, boxer shorts, socks and shoes in one clean sweep and leaving it by the bed till I pick it up next day.

♥

He leaves his clothes in a huge pile on a chair — the pile gets higher and higher until eventually they all fall off onto the floor.

♥

He leaves the wardrobe door and a drawer open and hangs his clothes from the drawer handles.

♥

The pile of ironed clothes waiting for him to put away are invisible to him.

♥

He leaves his towel draped over the door.

♥

He takes up most of the bed and the duvet and tosses and turns all night.

♥

He uses his laptop in bed.

♥

He picks his nails in bed. I found ten toenail clippings behind the bed. How disgusting is that!

After a night on the tiles

He came home this morning at his usual Hour of Four... he comes flounce into Bed, dead as a Salmon into a Fishmonger's Basket; his Feet cold as Ice, his Breath hot as a Furnace, and his Hands and his Face as greasy as his Flanel Night-cap. — Oh Matrimony! — He tosses up the Clothes with a barbarous swing over his Shoulders, disorders the whole Oeconomy of my Bed, leaves me half naked, and my whole Night's Comfort is the tuneable Serenade of that wakeful Nightingale, his Nose. — O the Pleasure of counting the

melancholy Clock by a snoring Husband!
**The Beaux Stratagem, George Farquhar
(1707)**

━━━━━━━━━◆━∾◦᪰━◆━━━━━━━━

And so to the other big bedroom issue... There you are, fast asleep, in the middle of a wonderful dream, when you are jolted awake by a sharp elbow in the ribs. 'You're snoring!' says the one with the sharp elbows. At 4am the chances of getting back to sleep are slender and the dream is irretrievable. The dig in the ribs was unnecessary. A normal snorer usually only snores when lying on his back, and so a gentle nudge is all that is needed to turn the snorer over without waking him. It's tough on the non-snorer who can't get back to sleep, but there's no point in two people tossing and turning, only to fall asleep just before the alarm clock goes off.

A really serious snorer, though, can make life miserable for the partner and even for the neighbours. I have stayed with friends where my host's snores cause the fabric of the house to vibrate. And, in cases like this, it may be as well to seek professional medical advice. Snoring is worse if you are overweight or a smoker, worse with a cold, and worse with alcohol or sleeping pills. Raising the head of the bed or piling up the pillows may help. I have also seen it suggested that one way to prevent someone sleeping on his back is to sew a tennis ball into the back of his pyjama top! One suffering wife writes, 'The snoring was a massive factor for us so we now have kind of fallen into sleeping apart. I miss our cuddles and chats.'

How Does Your Garden Grow?

> *In the end I moon about with Vita trying to convince her that planning is an element in gardening. I want to show her that the top of the moat-walk bank must be planted with forethought and design. She wishes just to jab in the things which she has left over. The tragedy of the romantic temperament is that it dislikes form so much that it ignores the effect of masses. She wants to put in stuff which 'will give a lovely red colour in the autumn.' I wish to put in stuff which will furnish shape to the perspective. In the end we part, not as friends.*
>
> **Harold Nicolson's Diary, 1946**
> **(published 1966)**

From Adam and Eve in the Garden of Eden, couples have shared the pleasures and pains of gardening. But a shared passion for the garden does not necessarily mean that all is sweetness and light. Vita Sackville-West and Harold Nicolson argued vehemently about their ideas for the garden at Sissinghurst, but out of dispute came perfection.

Another 20th-century garden writer, Margery Fish, had a husband who did not share her passion, and disapproved of her extravagance when tempted by new plants. Rather than confront Walter, she would waylay the postman and sneak parcels of plants into East Lambrook Manor when he was away from home. Walter's main use to her in the garden was as the owner of a sharp military sword which Margery used for slashing nettles.

The 18th-century novelist Fanny Burney and her husband, General D'Arblay, a refugee from the French Revolution, had a more harmonious gardening relation-ship. The General gardened with great enthusiasm, if little knowledge. He accidentally destroyed an asparagus bed, left a gap in the hedge wide enough for a herd of cattle to invade their cottage garden, and forgot to harvest his lettuces before they all bolted. And Fanny, gifted with an equable temperament and a sense of humour, saw their horticultural tribulations as a huge joke, and wrote sparkling letters describing them to her father.

For better, he says

It gives us real pleasure to garden together. We have a good system of division of labour and appreciate each other's work.

♥

She has created a wonderful garden. I just sit in a deck-chair with a drink beside me and a book, and enjoy it.

♥

She is the one with ideas and I am the doer. Would it be immodest to say we think the results are pretty good?

♥

She grows the most delicious vegetables.

For better, she says

He does it all, a very good job, neat, tidy and cheerful, not easy when you've got a mad dog!

♥

I leave it all to him. He makes the garden beautiful and I can look out and see beautiful flowers and eat wonderful veg.

♥

He makes the most beautiful supports for runner beans in the land.

♥

He tackles the bindweed and ivy, helps me unravel the hose pipe and cleans up; we're very happy working together in the garden.

For worse, he says

She spends far too much on plants and half of them die before she gets round to planting them.

♥

She doesn't want anything to do with the garden and takes no interest.

♥

She leaves little heaps of weeds lying on my lawn.

♥

When I offer to help, she tells me I don't know a seedling from a weed.

For worse, she says

He's only interested in the lawn and getting the mowing stripes exactly right. That, and edging. It takes all day but I must say it looks smart when he's finished.

♥

He prunes plants too ferociously. It's a miracle any of them survive.

♥

He orders endless weird plants from the internet, mostly completely unsuited to our soil and climate.

♥

He leaves bits of his boat strewn all over the garden, and then I have to pick them up before the children can play.

The smaller the garden, the more important it is for both partners to agree the layout and content, and as with interior decoration, the results are usually better if one partner is acknowledged to be in charge. In a large country garden, if a couple fail to reach agreement they can divide it into two. It's more difficult for creative spirits with conflicting ideas to be contained within the back yard of a town house.

Gavin's view of gardening [was] that he thought it very selfish of a man to have a garden larger than his wife could handle. My parents once asked if he wanted something for the garden for his birthday. 'Yes,' he said, 'six bags of concrete.'

Selective Memory, Katharine Whitehorn (2007)

Even in relatively large gardens, serious confrontations can happen. As a garden designer I sometimes need the skills of a marriage guidance counsellor. People call me in to adjudicate when they can't agree whether to cut a tree down or plant a hedge, or where to put the fish pond. I had one client who stamped her foot and threatened divorce over her partner's demand that she remove the creeper from the back of the house; and another who, when I suggested removing a group of ancient shrubs to open up a view, turned to his partner and said triumphantly, 'Told you so!'

Our own gardening relationship reached rock bottom over a large sycamore tree. Rob thought it did a good job screening the garden from neighbouring houses. I thought it cast too much shade and gave rise to endless tree seedlings that had to be weeded out. After two years of argument, I called in the tree surgeon when Rob was on a business trip. The head of the tree was removed, leaving a 10ft trunk which I planned to adorn with roses and clematis. 'He'll never notice,' I thought.

He noticed the moment he drove through the gate, and we didn't speak for days. He was right about the tree's function; I had opened up a clear view into our neighbour's bathroom. Luckily, sycamores are almost indestructible so, in spite of copious doses of poison, new branches soon sprang up. The Divorce Tree will soon be as big as it ever was.

When lesser disagreements occur, there's nothing like an hour's diligent weeding to restore one's good humour, and if this fails, a shed, the traditional male retreat, is a good place to retire to with one's grievance. Even gardens too small to accommodate a shed might have space for a Sulking Room, 'a nutshell of a summer house', as William Cowper described his, 'not much bigger than a sedan chair'. After a period of reflection aided by the scent of jasmine or honeysuckle, the crossest person might emerge with a smiling face.

Friction can often be avoided by respecting the traditional divisions of horticultural interests. People from Mars tend to enjoy planning the structure of the garden, leaving those from Venus to clothe the framework with pretty plants. His ambition is a lawn like a bowling green, and tidy rows of peas and beans, whereas her talent is expressed through flowering plants and her nurturing instinct is satisfied by sowing seeds and taking cuttings. The stereotypes often hold good.

Women report that their men mow, cut hedges and sweep up leaves. They grow delicious vegetables, but if let loose in the herbaceous border they line up the plants like soldiers. One man wishes his wife would cut the grass, but acknowledges that hay fever is a pretty good excuse. Another says his wife leaves tools lying where she last used them, to be discovered rusting away six months later. Apparently, women also leave little heaps of weeds lying around for someone else to clean up.

Appreciation is always more effective than criticism, and goes a long way towards bringing harmony to the garden. The flower gardener knows perfectly well when there is a sad lack of colour in the borders (usually at the end of July and beginning of August), and resents having it pointed out. Better to say, 'I like those blue things; can we have more of them next year?'

And, at times when the garden delights the eye, don't just think it, say it. After all, as Sydney Eddison put it: 'Gardens are a form of autobiography.'

People from Mars tend to enjoy planning the structure of the garden, leaving those from Venus to clothe the framework with pretty plants.

PRE-AIRPORT TENSION

Sheila I'll get the papers and aspirins too.

Frederick You'll miss the plane, I keep telling you.

Sheila I need some eau-de-cologne and scent.

Frederick But what would you say if the dashed plane went?

Sheila I want some coffee. I'll phone my aunt.

Frederick I'll see to the tickets. I really can't stand more of
your wanting this and that.

Sheila I've just remembered, I need a hat!

Frederick Passport, currency, baggage check…

Sheila I look – Oh God – a perfect wreck!

Frederick I'd best insure, and check the time.

Sheila What I want is a gin and lime.

(The flight is called)

Sheila I like to sit right in the tail –

Frederick The forward seats are always best.

Sheila - in case the engines all should fail.

Frederick You've put it, have you, to the test?

Sheila I'll want to read. You'll want to sleep.

Frederick You'll want to smoke. I hate the smell.

Sheila Your selfishness will make me weep.

Frederick I think this flight is utter hell!

C. Northcote Parkinson

3
OUT AND ABOUT

Kings of the Road

The Hadleys are setting off on holiday. Tempers are frayed. Mum has loaded two suitcases into the car boot, then her big pasta saucepan, filled with essential groceries, soap and loo paper. Dad takes everything out again and puts it back in exactly the same place, adding the rest of the holiday paraphernalia, and finally the toddler's buggy. The boot won't shut, so everything is packed a third time.

Finally they're off, Dad in the driving seat. He zeroes the milometer and looks at his watch.

'10.23. Write that down, will you?' he says.

'I don't need to write the time down to know we're leaving 20 minutes late.'

'We wouldn't be if you hadn't spent hours on the phone to your mother and then thrown everything willy-nilly into the boot so I had to repack it…'

'Oh, it's my fault, of course. Look out! He's turning right.'

'I can see what he's doing. Did you pick up my suit from the cleaners?'

Yikes. She didn't. Time to counter-attack. 'This is a 40-mile-an-hour limit, remember. You don't want more points on your licence, do you?'

And so it goes on, each thinking up annoying things to say to the other until the children's bickering eclipses theirs. After a couple of hours on the road, they stop at a lacklustre motorway service station. Lunch, cynically presented and priced, puts them in a worse mood.

He feels tired, so she drives for a bit. Instead of letting him sleep, she can't resist saying, 'I told you we should have brought a picnic. It's such a lovely day.'

'Oh for heaven's sake. We just want to get on with the journey and get there.'

Ten minutes later, she brakes suddenly. 'Look out!' he shouts. 'What the hell are you doing? You didn't even see that lorry!'

'I did see the lorry,' she says, icily. 'That's why I braked.'

'You left it bloody late. You never anticipate, that's your trouble. It's a wonder we ever get anywhere in one piece.'

'If I'm so dangerous,' she says, pulling over on to the hard shoulder and braking hard again. '*You* drive.'

For some couples even the shortest car journey can be fraught. Punctuality may be the first issue (the one who insists on watering all the plants just before leaving, and the other who goes back into the house to give the shoes a quick polish each test their partner's patience to breaking point), but the trouble with driving and cars is that there are seemingly endless possibilities for tension – if we are not arguing over each other's driving skills, it's our navigation skills or one or the other's objectionable concept of vehicle etiquette…

WOMEN DRIVERS!

Never call a woman a lousy driver. It is likely to make her crash, say psychologists at Queensland University, Australia. Women who are told that men are much better drivers are more than twice as likely to collide with jaywalking pedestrians, Dr Courtney von Hippel reports in Accident Analysis and Prevention. She says that when people are confronted with negative stereotypes about themselves, it can harm their performance. Women drivers face this a lot, she adds, such as seeing men shaking their heads when they try to reverse into a space.

Daily Telegraph, 8 November 2005

Everyone gets upset if their driving is criticised – although women drivers, are, like mothers-in-law, apparently supposed to accept criticism without comment. We are constantly being told that we are incapable of backing into a parking space, and can't help but use the brakes to slow down when a man would do it with a gear change. And yet many women think they are rather better drivers than their partners, and feel mildly peeved that the fact goes unacknowledged.

To criticise a man's driving, on the other hand, is tantamount to questioning his virility. If a partner's driving really is alarming, the subject should be broached with immense tact – and not when in the car. If the conversation can be prompted by an event such as a friend being had up for speeding, or narrowly escaping an accident, so much the better. Emphasise concern for the safety of your beloved and try not to use any of the Red Card phrases: 'You always…'; 'You never…', 'Why don't you…?' I have to admit that the chances of developing a rational discussion are slender and, if there is a bad reaction, there's no point in allowing the exchange to turn into a full-blown row. Having wounded his self-esteem, it's best to drop the topic and find a way to bolster his ego instead. The driver will have got the message.

Nothing, however, causes quite so much trouble as the vexed area of navigation. This is one of those Mars-Venus problems, with men routinely wheeling out their belief that women are wired up differently – and have little spa-

*For some couples even the shortest
car journey can be fraught.*

tial awareness. 'She's completely clueless with any map,' grumbles one husband. 'She actually turns it round when navigating!' Well, for heaven's sake, how else can we tell left from right when travelling in any direction other than due north?

'She', who has unwillingly had the role of map-reader thrust upon her in the first place, will, of course, trade punch for punch. The driver, she says, is bad at following directions, and goes so fast she can't read the road signs. 'I have to be constantly on the alert or he'll miss a turning. He won't trust me when we're on the road. I say "Take the next left" and he says "Are you sure?" which undermines my confidence, and by the time I've checked on the map again, we've overshot the turning. It's been happening for 44 years.'

A friend, who's been married nearly as long as Rob and I, solved the problem by giving her husband a satellite navigation kit for his 60th birthday. They agree that the present came just in time to avoid divorce – apparently the voice of the lady in the dashboard is less annoying than his wife's. One in five drivers now use Sat Nav, so perhaps one in five marriages under threat will be saved. When the car ends up at the bottom of a lane leading into a field of cattle, at least the Sat Nav can be blamed rather than the Old Bat Nav.

Much of the trouble between couples in cars comes down to the fact that neither party can bear to lose face – although men seem to be worse on this score. According to a survey carried out for the RAC, British male drivers waste a total of 5.9 million hours each year by not admitting they are lost, and wait an average of 20 minutes before stopping to get directions, compared with women drivers who wait a mere ten. To ask the way is to admit defeat. It seems that men would rather drive in ever-increasing circles, getting further and further from their destination, than ask for help.

'Because research shows that men generally have better spatial skills than women,' says the survey, 'when it comes to map-reading and navigating there's added pressure on them to perform well.'

'Asking for directions,' the RAC advises, 'is in no way an admission of inadequacy.' Just don't quote that to your partner when approaching a crossroad where the arms of the signpost have been snapped off, in a country lane with grass growing down the middle. If he finally admits it's a good idea to ask at the cottage on the corner, he is still not going to be seen doing the asking. 'You go and ask,' he'll say, 'while I turn the car round.'

For worse, she says

He's like Mr Toad as soon as he gets behind the wheel. He jumps into gaps that are too small, takes risks, and goes much too fast round bends, making everybody car sick.

♥

He goes far too fast. I've been known to end up lying, a gibbering wreck, on the floor of the car.

He won't fill up with petrol till past the last moment. Three times we've run out.

♥

Talk about the pot calling the kettle black! He accuses me of bad driving, but he's really terrible himself, not just a bad driver but actually dangerous.

♥

He has alarming attacks of road rage. I live in fear that one day someone is going to get out of their car and throttle him.

♥

He answers his mobile on the motorway at 80mph and proceeds to conduct a business meeting.

♥

He can't talk and drive at the same time, so if we have a conversation in the car, he slows down to about 50mph and it takes for ever to get where we're going.

♥

He likes the air-conditioning set at freezing.

For worse, he says

When she borrows my car, she never puts things back the way she found them. The driver's seat is adjusted so my knees hit my chin; she's fiddled with the mirror and the heating controls and has somehow tuned into a Welsh-language radio station.

♥

She drives far too close to the car in front — so does my

mother. I think all women do it.

♥

She never budges out of the middle lane, just sits there letting the world go by on either side.

♥

She has the heating on full blast, like a hairdryer, and endlessly flicks from one radio station to another.

But journeys by car don't have to be a test of your patience. A long drive provides a rare opportunity for conversation and, for couples who lead busy lives, it may be their only chance to discuss what to do about Granny, or whether to move Johnnie to another school. It's also a good time for more light-hearted exchanges of gossip about friends and colleagues, or jokes heard at work. Or simply a chance to listen to a grown-up programme on the radio or a favourite CD.

Nor should the car itself be allowed to become a battle zone. We all know one or two drivers who, not content with having delightful children, a puppy and a kitten to love, develop an unhealthy relationship with their car, washing, cleaning and grooming it obsessively. They are to be pitied, because it's a sad fact of life that, just when the body work is freshly waxed and gleaming, a pigeon will fly over. And, if a pile of drinks cans, apple cores, crumbs and chocolate wrappers accumulates, and sticky fingers have spoiled the once-spotless upholstery, they should take what comfort there is from the thought that it's easier to change a car than to change one's children.

Still, as my husband knows from experience, nothing is so sorely trying as living with an obsessive gardener who fills the car to the gunnels with booty from plant sales and garden centres. When compost escapes into the car, the partner tries not to complain, but patience may give out when, in search of a missing credit card, grass is found to be growing underneath the driver's seat.

*Most families now talk more
in the car than at home.*
Office for National Statistics

For better in the car, he says
When she's not pregnant, she's a very good driver, the only person I can stand being driven by, actually.

♥

She goes to sleep so I can have my own choice of music.

♥

She chats, keeps the kids entertained, hands me a drink, supplies me with Murray Mints, and takes over the driving when I'm tired.

♥

When we go out to dinner she doesn't drink and does drive.

For better in the car, she says

He's a safe, excellent driver, and a good route planner. I just leave the whole journey to him, while I knit or snooze.

♥

He always knows how to get where he's going even when I'm supposed to be map-reading. Just as well, because I only have to take one look at the map and I get car sick.

♥

When I drive he simply falls asleep, so I'm never nervous that he'll criticise me.

♥

I don't drive and he goes 30 minutes out of his way to take me to work and pick me up, and never complains about it.

Retail Therapy

> *Don't always refuse to go shopping with your wife. Of course it's a nuisance but sometimes she honestly wants your advice, and you ought to be pleased to give it.*
>
> **Don'ts for Husbands, Blanche Ebbutt (1913)**

Don't take your husband on a laborious shopping expedition and expect him to remain good-tempered throughout.
Don'ts for Wives, Blanche Ebbutt (1913)

There's a myth about shopping – that it is the favourite occupation of all women. But actually it is not the shopping itself that women love – shopping alone, even for clothes, is not that much fun – it is the meeting up with a friend that counts, the having someone there to gawp at designer handbags, steer us away from the neon pink sequinned top with the daring cleavage, and say, 'yes, your bum does look horrendously big in that'. The shopping is just an excuse. It's what Venus does while Mars is watching football.

She always does look nicely dressed. We always look at some of our neighbours and say, 'Fancy going down the road looking like that.' But Betty wouldn't, she would have to dress up – just to fetch a tin of beans.
The English Marriage, Drusilla Beyfus (1968)

No two partners are quite the same. One husband 'enjoys shopping with me, even for shoes'. Another 'carries the shopping, is good fun and not obsessed with money, happy to spend it on either of us, not just on what he wants'; a third is 'good at picking clothes for me'. But genuine male shopping enthusiasts are rare. The majority of couples only shop together on holiday, when he can't escape, or when a major household item, such as a bed or a dishwasher, is needed. Even on holiday the husband who 'follows me round looking bored till I give in and go for a drink' is the norm.

For better, he says

She doesn't expect me to go with her, which suits me: I'd be a misery.

♥

She has beautiful taste and bullies me into buying nice clothes.

♥

I provide encouragement and advice when she's clothes shopping, and she seems happy to take it, which is very gratifying!

♥

When shopping together, as in all other aspects of life, she's the least selfish person I've ever met.

For better, she says

He buys treats for me like chocolate and sometimes

surprises me with very nice presents.

♥

He makes the effort to buy me fair-trade flowers.

♥

He's fab for clothes shopping, bags of taste and patience, and shops at a perfect pace, never hurrying me.

♥

He loves shopping for food. I can leave the weekly shop entirely to him.

♥

At the supermarket he pushes the trolley and amuses the baby.

♥

When I get back from shopping he dashes out to help unload the heavy groceries.

For worse, he says

If she sees the perfect thing immediately she won't get it until she's spent the rest of the morning looking to make sure there's nothing better.

♥

She wants to buy as quickly as possible — I like to consider alternatives.

♥

She spends hours stopping and gazing at things we don't want to buy.

♥

She's wildly extravagant with all kinds of shopping: food, clothes, and things for the house.

For worse, she says

He tells me the first dress I try on is perfect when it defi-nitely is not.

♥

He gets seduced by multi-buy offers: so we have loads of stuff we don't get round to eating before it goes off.

♥

He buys things for the children when I've said no, like sweets and biscuits.

♥

If he goes shopping it's a disaster. He returns with jars of Nutella, packets of crisps, miso soup, Penguins, and yet another packet of prunes. They sit around until they're past their sell-by date — often for years. Nothing I can actually cook for dinner.

Shopping for clothes is a relatively infrequent occurrence, but shopping for food is a weekly necessity, and, as it has to be done, it might as well be done efficiently and pleasurably.

In theory at least, when two people shop together, the load halves and the process speeds up. For keen foodies shopping is never a chore to be got through as quickly as possible. It's a pleasure to be shared, both tasting and testing at each stall or counter, enjoying the discovery of new ingredients and combinations.

The secret of harmonious shopping is the list. Without it couples risk blocking the supermarket aisle while they have a heated argument about whether there are enough yoghurts in the fridge to last the weekend. Back in the kitchen, having unpacked the shopping, they blame each other for forgetting to buy milk. Lists are more fun if made together with a recipe book to hand, as a reminder of what is needed for a favourite dish, and as an incentive to try something new.

However, shopping as a team doesn't work for everyone, and many women prefer to get on with it without the distraction of a companion. Any man found shopping alone in a supermarket is usually there under duress and the general consensus is that men can't be trusted to come home with what they set out to get. There are a few notable exceptions. I am married to one. I'm eternally grateful to a friend who ran a very successful retail business and introduced Rob to the idea that shops and shopping of all kinds are fascinating. As a result I seldom have to do the day-to-day shopping. He sallies forth, armed with a list that has gradually built up on a blackboard in the kitchen. Occasionally the list gets lost between home and the shops, but midweek, it's so short he can write it on his hand. On one occasion, in our local Co-op, he found the ink on his hand had smudged and he was unable to read his own blurred handwriting. The checkout lady and two customers, eager to help, pored over his palm like fortune-tellers, and eventually were able to decipher the words 'chicken, garlic, cream'.

Travel Fever

Don't take a house for your summer holiday unless your family is so large that you are obliged to. It is no holiday for your wife to have to do her housekeeping — and probably under less convenient conditions — in another town or village. If you must do it, take her to a boarding house or hotel another time to give her a complete holiday.
Don'ts for Husbands, Blanche Ebbutt (1913)

If he thinks he would like a week's walking tour with you as a chum, don't object that it may rain, or that you haven't a suitable dress, or that you can't manage for a week with nothing in the way of luggage except a nightdress and a toothbrush. Enter into the spirit of the thing.
Don'ts for Wives, Blanche Ebbutt (1913)

The anticipation of a holiday can be almost as good as the holiday itself. When life gets stressful, the thought of that precious time away can be the one thing that keeps us sane. The knowledge that there will soon be nothing to do except eat, drink and generally enjoy each others' company can get couples through a bad patch at work, and stop them yelling at the children or kicking the washing machine.

But it's small wonder that a holiday together, like a family Christmas, can be a marital flashpoint. The more we fantasise about the longed-for break, the more likely we are to be disappointed by the reality. At the marriage counselling agency Relate, the queue for relationship advice gets longer in September, after the summer holidays, and again in January, after Christmas.

According to Relate's spokesperson, a holiday, far from being a magic cure for matrimonial ills, is a crucible for any relationship: all the ingredients are there and then they are heated up. It's not the holiday that creates the problems, but it doesn't solve them either. Instead, it highlights them because when we are away and everything is supposed to be perfect, the usual excuses, like 'I'm under a lot of stress at work' or 'The baby kept me awake half the night', just won't wash.

For worse, he says
She's indecisive so I always have to take the initiative. It can be annoying when she won't say where she'd like to eat, or what time, but on the whole we like doing the same things so we do have a good time together.

♥

I wish she would be more relaxed. She's always fretting about whether everything's all right at home.

♥

She's in charge of the camera but takes very few pictures then never gets round to downloading them.

♥

She never takes my advice about putting on sunscreen and then whinges when she gets sunburned.

For worse, she says

We haven't had a proper holiday for eight years, mainly because he won't commit to plans.

♥

He sees the world entirely through a camera lens, and is always saying 'just go and stand over there'.

♥

He's usually so tired from work that he's ill on holiday the first few days. After that we do enjoy ourselves — just pottering about and having fine wine and food.

♥

He likes to explore and I like to sunbathe so we try to do both but it annoyed me when we booked a hot holiday in Tenerife and he spent the whole time in the shade looking miserable.

♥

He's gregarious to a fault. I like to relax, just the two of us, and have romantic dinners in the evenings, but he invites everyone he meets to join us.

The secret to a successful holiday that doesn't have us rushing to sign up for marriage guidance as soon as we get home is to prepare for it mentally and emotionally, as well as practically. Being on holiday won't change anyone's personality. On the contrary, a long period of unaccustomed daily proximity will throw the things that irritate us into sharper relief. So it's best to accept them for what they are: minor irritations that we cannot change. And can we admit, too, that, for every annoying habit of theirs, we have an equally annoying one?

For better, he says

We agree on where to go, and like the same things: good food and wine, lovely scenery, not over-cultural.

♥

I'm quite bossy when planning the sightseeing and the route, but she doesn't mind and is brilliant to be with as she's so relaxed and easy-going.

♥

She digests the guidebooks for me and chooses the food, and I walk and drink in the atmosphere and liquor.

♥

We love our holidays. We travel very well together and get very involved with everything and everyone.

For better, she says

He takes charge and I agree to almost everything as he's so

good at getting us to interesting places. I just love
being looked after — he gets taxis, does the ordering in
restaurants and I can relax completely.

♥

We're very compatible, both lazy and like doing nothing;
we just relax and go with the flow.

♥

He's excellent at planning sightseeing, and organises
our travelling perfectly. He books everything, but I don't
let him near the passports for fear he'll lose them. I leave
everything else to him, except for sometimes saying enough
is enough… no more cathedrals! We have evolved a rule
that works quite well: 'seen one… seen them all.' It can be
applied to cathedrals, Roman amphitheatres, stalactites;
you name it.

♥.

He's great at chatting to the locals, which makes us feel
more like travellers, less like tourists.

The importance of communication is a recurrent theme
in this book, and a holiday may be the one time in the
year when we have each other's undivided attention, and a
chance to talk honestly about our relationship as a couple,
or our family life. It would be difficult to overemphasise
the importance of finding time to be alone together, even
if it's only for an occasional weekend in which to unwind
and relax, and to rediscover how loving and close and
comfortable you feel together.

A holiday alone can also provide the best atmosphere for discussing important matters and making difficult decisions. The problem may be whether to have your father-in-law to live with you, whether to go back to work or how to improve your sex life. It will be easier to solve when the constraints and distractions of work and family life are removed and reaching a decision will make the rest of the holiday a carefree, happy time.

So, if you're wondering how you can possibly leave the children to have quality time together, don't! Just go ahead and do it. Now is the time to draw on the bank of goodwill you have built up with your parents and in-laws.

The decision about where to go may well have to be dictated by children's term times and the bank balance. But even when time and money are not a problem, there is no guarantee that a couple will share each other's idea of a dream holiday. One person may long to go trekking in the Himalayas, while their partner dreams of lying beside a swimming pool in the South of France, sipping a glass of cold Chablis and chatting to friends.

Separate holidays work for some couples. One partner can hold the fort at home while the other goes off alone or with a friend. There may be beneficial side effects: increased self-confidence for someone who has grown to rely too much on their partner's support; broadened horizons, making each person better company as well as more independent; and new friendships to share.

If separate holidays are the answer, make them short

and set aside the time and the money for a shared holiday as well.

And, remember, there's nothing like being generous to make yourself feel good. So concentrate on making the holiday fun for the other person.

When out sightseeing in the city, notice that your partner is wilting before there is a complaint, and make out that it is you who wants to stop at the next café for a cold drink. The frescoes in the chapel can wait.

The first few items on the Holiday Checklist opposite may seem painfully obvious, but believe me they are easily missed, or left too late. It nearly happened to us. Our last holiday was a trip to St Petersburg with some friends. Months in advance we sent our passports to be stamped with a visa for Russia, and back they came. The day before departure I looked in the passport drawer in my desk. No passports. Suppressing rising panic, we searched the house, turning it upside down and inside out; to no avail. In a state of calm despair, we went through all the possibilities.

Last time we had used the passports had been on a weekend visit to Jersey a month earlier. Had we left the passports there? After a phone call and an exhaustive search at the other end, the answer was no.

HOLIDAY CHECKLIST

- Book flights! ☺
- REX → kennels? in-laws?
- PASSPORTS — do we need visas?
- HIRE CAR | use voucher |
- BANK: get Euros/ Rupees/Roubles
- SUN TAN CREAM (factor 6 for R, 25 for me)
- BOOKS & MAGS
- BIKINI
- SARONG
- Mobiles & ADAPTOR PLUGS
- phone Mrs P. re cat
- KEY: put under flowerpot in greenhouse.

Was 24 hours long enough to get to the Passport Office in London to replace the lost passports? Perhaps.

Would there then be time to go to the Russian embassy and get a new visa? No. It takes a week.

After the trip to Jersey we'd driven home from the airport. Were the passports still in the car? In the glove compartment? Under the seat? No.

We were on the point of ringing our travelling companions to say that we weren't going to join them the next morning, when a bit of lateral thinking led us to the airport car park we'd used when we flew to Jersey. We rang them. Yes, yes, yes! Two passports had been left on the desk in the office a month ago. Left by whom? Best not to ask.

Don't Forget Your Toothbrush

> *For many women the real point about marriage is to have someone to carry their bags… If you're going to stay married, for God's sake travel separately.*
>
> **The Grumpy Man's Guide to Marriage,**
> **Eric Idle**

With us it's the other way round. My husband is the one who ought to be married to a good old-fashioned porter, while I'm the one who likes to travel light. We have resolved our differences by, whenever possible, packing all our stuff in one big suitcase – which Rob has to carry.

Sharing a suitcase, however, can be as divisive as loading the dishwasher. One husband favours the army method, maximising available space by stuffing socks and hankies into shoes, and avoiding creases by rolling clothes up instead of folding them. His wife, probably a lady's maid in a previous incarnation, uses linen shoe bags and reams of tissue paper.

For us, packing can never be considered complete until the car is beyond the turning-back zone – about three miles from home. Until we've passed the King's Arms, there's still time to go back for something we've forgotten: washing things, perhaps, or the present for the hosts. Beyond this point, there's no use in even asking 'Did you pack...?' unless we are spoiling for a fight or essentials have been left behind – passports, wallet or glasses.

Travelling Hopefully

Some people have a relaxed attitude to catching planes or trains. To them, time spent hanging about at an airport or station is time wasted, and they like to show up just before the final call for their flight. My husband is like this. He used to consider it a personal triumph to arrive at the station in time to board a train just as the wheels began to roll. The annoying thing was that it always seemed to work, and he never missed a train until the day

British Rail began locking the doors 30 seconds before the train's departure. But this is not a system that works for me. I'm of the opposite persuasion and am more likely to end up catching the train before the one I planned on catching. For weekends away I used to arrive at the station with luggage, toddler and carrycot a good half-hour before ETD, then spend the waiting time in a frenzy of nerves, scanning the horizon for my nonchalant husband.

Train fever

July 17th. — Robert sees me off [to Paris] by early train for London, after scrambled and agitating departure, exclusively concerned with frantic endeavours to induce suitcase to shut. This is at last accomplished, but leaves me with conviction that it will be at least equally difficult to induce it to open again. Vicky bids me cheerful, but affectionate good-bye and then shatters me at eleventh hour by enquiring trustfully if I shall be home in time to read to her after tea?…

Arrive at station too early — as usual — and I fill in time by asking Robert if he will telegraph if anything happens to the children, as I could be back again in twenty-four hours. He only enquires in return whether I have my passport? Am perfectly aware that passport is in my small purple dressing-case, where I put it a week ago, and have looked at it two or three times every day ever since — last time just before leaving my room forty-five minutes ago. Am nevertheless mysteriously impelled to open handbag, take out key, unlock small purple dressing-case, and verify presence of passport all over again...

Arrival of train, and I say goodbye to Robert, and madly enquire if he would rather I gave up going at all? He rightly ignores this altogether.

Diary of a Provincial Lady, E.M. Delafield (1947)

———————⚮———————

It's strange how often sufferers from Train Fever end up living with last-minuters. If only there was a pill we could take before we set out which would put us into a dreamless sleep until we arrive at our destination. As it is, the fretter will never persuade the nonchalant one to change his ways, and must go through agony every time they travel together.

'Are We There Yet?'

Going on holiday with children is best treated as a holiday for the children only. Parents who think it can be a holiday for them as well are doomed to disappointment. Conversely, if they work at making the holiday fun for their children, they may find they quite enjoy it.

It can help to share holidays with close friends or to import a couple of grandparents as childminders and babysitters for part of the holiday.

———— ◆ ᘒ•ᘖ ◆ ————

We had an awful lot of fuss and preparation getting away in the first place. When we got there either one boy was fed up because he wanted to go roller-skating, or our other son was fed up because he wanted to go swimming and nobody else did, and Debs was fed up because there was nothing to do in the evenings and I was fed up because I didn't want to be dragged here, there and everywhere. I'd rather rough it a bit, go camping, perhaps. Next year I'll take the boys on my own, or go by myself.

The English Marriage, **Drusilla Beyfus (1968)**

———— ◆ ᘒ•ᘖ ◆ ————

A few tips for the journey... Before a long car ride, it's worth planning a lunch stop away from the motorway. There's nothing restful about queuing for a sub-standard, overpriced motorway services meal, then having to drag the children away from sweet shelves or slot machines. It will put the whole family in a bad mood. If, on the other hand, there is a good lunch and a little gentle sightseeing en route, instead of a frustrating wasted day, the journey becomes part of the holiday. So plan a short diversion to a pub in a pretty village, or a National Trust garden with a café. A good meal, an amble round the garden or down a country lane, a short snooze in the sun, and we go on our way refreshed.

While *en route*, keep children happy with frequent stops. At moments of crisis, dish out drinks and snacks, and intersperse listening to music or stories with games everyone can join in, like 'I Spy'. The games may bore adults rigid, but playing them is preferable to listening to bickering in the back seat. Set a good example by refraining from joining in the squabbles about who cheated.

Back to Earth with a Bump

Whether the holiday is an unqualified success, or, as sometimes happens, the obligation to show a happy front has put a strain on the relationship, returning home may be an anti-climax; that brief moment of truth when we walk into the house after an absence and see it with the eyes of a stranger can bring on a feeling of mild depression. It's shabbier than one remembers, there's a funny smell in the kitchen and a dog to fetch from the kennels. Then there is the need to phone Mother to tell her what a great time was had, the washing, organising oneself to go back to work, sorting out school uniforms and lunch boxes. This mild depression is a completely normal reaction and will disappear once we are back in the swing of family life.

THE FIANCÉE

'Well, what did you think of her?'

'Of course, they've all got this terrific poise nowadays, haven't they?'

'Yes, I noticed that too. But I quite liked her.'

'Oh, I quite liked her too. The hat was a mistake.'

'The hat was a mistake but the frock was good. Would you say it was a perm, or natural, when she took off her hat?'

'A frightfully good perm.'.....

'I must say, I never thought Tony would choose that kind of wife, did you? I mean – well – she's so sort of tall, isn't she?'

'Oh huge. Though I must say she's got good eyes. Naturally, Tony's my only son, and I feel very, very anxious about the future. I've always said that my children must go their own way; no one can ever say I've interfered with them, and I'm not going to say one word now.'

'Mother, do you think she's frightful?'

'No dear, I don't want to say that. I'm old-fashioned, I suppose. To my mind, a man must choose his wife for himself, without advice from anybody. As I said to Tony before he ever proposed to this girl: Make sure that she's good, and a lady, and healthy, and intelligent, and that she's going to get on with your friends and relations, and you with hers – and then, my dear boy, if you feel that you can afford to marry – then I suppose there's no help for it.'

Article in *Punch* by E.M. Delafield
(1890-1943)

4

FAMILY MATTERS

The family — that dear octopus from whose tentacles we never quite escape, nor, in our inmost hearts, ever quite wish to.
Dodie Smith (1896–1990)

A family is a unit composed not only of children but of men, women, an occasional animal, and the common cold.
Ogden Nash (1902–1971)

'Love me, love my family' may not be spoken in so many words, but it is understood by both parties in any marriage. We all want to have a happy relationship with each other's parents and siblings, and are glad to see them from time to time. It just isn't always *convenient*.

As with so many aspects of married life, these things cut both ways. There is simply no point in protesting that you went there only two Sundays ago and your children spent the whole journey bickering. Unless you have a cast-iron excuse you should go, simply because you are now one of their family. As *they* are of *yours*.

Besides, always look on the bright side, as the song goes. Perhaps your mother-in-law's cooking will have miraculously improved and your careful father-in-law be a little more liberal with the drink. Perhaps your sister-in-law will take the children aside and play a game with them so you can relax and enjoy an uninterrupted conversation with your brother-in-law, who turns out to be more fun than you realised.

Perhaps not, of course. But at the worst, even if the food is vile, the drink non-existent and the children break their truce within the first half-mile, you will leave your parents-in-laws' house with a warm feeling that you have done your duty.

Meet the Parents

The first encounters with a partner's family can be nerve-racking. When I first met my mother-in-law, I was, for no good reason, in awe of her, and after I'd been married to her son for five years, and we'd become very fond of each other, she admitted to me, 'I thought you would be snooty.'

The way people react when a potential new family

member appears on the scene varies enormously and doesn't necessarily set the scene for the future. In close families, a new boyfriend or girlfriend may be produced for scrutiny early in the relationship. It's unnerving for the new boyfriend to sit at the family table, grilled by the father as to his background and job prospects, force-fed by the mother with second helpings he's too polite to refuse, and gawped at unblinkingly by young siblings. Anyone who can face the ordeal a second time must be truly smitten. But by the second and third occasion everyone is more relaxed and soon the boyfriend begins to feel at home.

At the other end of the scale, relationships may be kept secret from the parents and siblings so that, when a son finally gets round to producing a girlfriend in public, the family's suppressed excitement is hard to conceal. Mustering all his thespian powers to act casual, he says, 'Oh by the way, is it OK if a friend comes to lunch on Sunday?'

'Fine, what's his name?'

'Er... it's a her. Lauren.'

His parents try not to exchange significant glances, and by now their expectations are so high that they are almost sure to be disappointed.

Certainly, there are some families we would be crazy to consider marrying into unless we were truly, madly, deeply in love. In *Pride and Prejudice*, Mr Darcy regarded the Bennet family as nightmare in-laws, but he was so in love with Elizabeth that he was prepared to marry her in spite of them. Unfortunately, tact was not his strong suit, and he made the mistake of letting her know what he thought of them.

'The situation of your mother's family,' wrote Darcy to Elizabeth [her mother's brother was not a country gentleman but worked in the City], 'though objectionable, was nothing in comparison of that total want of propriety so frequently, so almost uniformly betrayed by herself, by your three younger sisters, and occasionally even by your father.'

Undine Spragg in Edith Wharton's *The Custom of the Country* is as big a snob as Mr Darcy. When her aristocratic French brother-in-law decides to marry Looty Arlington, an American girl he met at a skating rink, Undine decides, 'She must be horribly common.' She is uneasily aware that her own husband, Elmer Moffatt, a rich industrialist from out west, is considered, in the social set she aspires to, 'not a gentleman', and soon becomes disillusioned, complaining about his 'loudness and redness, his misplaced joviality, his familiarity with the servants and his habit of leaving old newspapers about the drawing room'.

Undine sees marriage as a convenient way to climb a rung of the social ladder, and regards divorce in the same light: 'He isn't in the right set,' she says of a friend's husband, 'and I think Mabel realises she'll never really get anywhere till she gets rid of him.'

--- ✦ ✦ ---

A tricky sister-in-law

Hee [the letter-writer's husband, Mr Dury]
hath such a sistir as is soe intolerable, and hee
is so wrought upon by her impudence... I can-
not apprehend less than that shee will make
my whole life unhapie and unserviceable to
mr Durey and others if I must live nearer her,
what I should doe I know not, the lord give me
strength to do my duty notwithstanding all
difficulties and opposition: I wish you could take
notice of the lowdnes of her toungue against
mee...

**Letter from Dorothy Moore to Samuel
Hartlib 30 January 1645**

--- ✦ ✦ ---

It's naive to assume parents and siblings will feel exactly
the same way about the love of our lives as we do. Parents
tend to feel nobody is good enough for their darling, but
they need to keep their feelings at bay. At their peril do
they put their child into a position of choosing between
family and love, for when push comes to shove, if the relationship is serious and long-term, the child's first loyalty
will be towards the partner.

My mother ticked me off when, announcing to my parents that Rob and I were engaged, I said, 'I hope you like
him.' 'You shouldn't care,' my mother told me, 'whether

we like him or not, if you truly love him.' They did like him, but I'm sure her advice to other parents would have been fairly uncompromising: once you are sure the relationship is permanent, you need to put aside any misgivings and find qualities to like in the new partner. A child has a right to expect loyalty in this respect, even if it's not always forthcoming.

An 80-year-old woman described to me how her marriage, which lasted 40 years, had been put at risk by her own mother's attitude. From the day she had introduced her future spouse to her, her mother, a strong personality, had made it only too clear that she felt her daughter could have chosen better. The daughter, instead of sticking up for her husband against the constant criticism meted out by her mother, meekly put up with it, and suffered in silence when her mother snubbed him in front of the rest of the family. As a result, the only prolonged periods of happiness in her marriage came when her husband was working abroad and they lived out of reach of her mother's influence. She may sound a bit weak, but it's surprising how many people, tough in other respects, find it difficult to defy their parents.

It's important, from the start, not to tolerate snide remarks to or about a partner from members of our own family, even at the risk of seeming ridiculously sensitive or lacking in a sense of humour. Most reasonable people will get the message and start treating the relationship as something genuine and permanent. The last thing most parents want is to drive a child away by making the chosen partner unwelcome, and if their attitude seems less than friendly it's more likely due to thoughtlessness than malice. Give both sets of parents time to adjust to the relationship.

Mary did not mind that his hat was rather small and un-English, because it was such fun to be with him. All the same, she could not help saying: 'Why don't you take your hat off and let the sun get at your hair? It's good for it.' She felt somehow that by removing the hat she could remove all the other tiny things which had not mattered at all in Paris, and which ought not to matter here. She wanted everyone else to think him perfect, and more than anything she wanted to think him perfect herself, never to have even the smallest disloyal doubt...
[Later they meet her cousin Denys, the object of her childhood and teenage adoration...]

As they shook hands, the contrast between him and Pierre in his pointed shoes made Mary not want to look at them. This mustn't happen. She mustn't think like this... Pierre did not look right in the country...

Mariana, Monica Dickens (1940)

At the same time, you and your spouse must try to be

flexible and to fit in as well as you each can with the new in-laws on either side. No family is a carbon copy of any other family. And both of yours will have their problem members and their share of eccentrics. They will have their own rules of behaviour, their private jokes and their own ways of expressing (or not) their affection. Accept them for what they are, and be aware that it will take time to get to know each other. It's natural for them to regard someone new with suspicion until they can be sure that it is a happy relationship. If there is a particular bond with one parent or favourite sibling, then there may also, initially, be jealousy to contend with.

Most important of all, though: if there are problems, don't try to solve them by attempting to be the kind of person that seems acceptable to them. It wasn't that person that your partner fell in love with, it was you, so be yourself and give it time.

For better, he says
My family all think she's great and she's very fond
of my parents but she doesn't like visits to last too long,

♥

I'm amazed how she takes her own family for granted.
They seem very special to me, they're exceptionally warm-
hearted, and make me feel as if I belong.

♥

I come from a big, chaotic family and she only has her
parents, so they make a big fuss of me, and I enjoy that.

My wife's very good at reminding me to phone my elderly father every Sunday. If it were left to me I would often forget.

For better, she says

He finds my family easier to get on with than his own. They think he's wonderful, sensible (unlike me) and I'm lucky to have found him.

♥

My dad thinks the world of him, I know he's my dad's favourite son-in-law and I'm really glad because I care what Dad thinks.

♥

There have been some soap-opera situations in my family and my husband deserves a medal for never losing his rag!

♥

He helps me and my brother see eye to eye (we used to fight a lot), and is always ready to give my dad a hand.

For worse, he says

My parents are divorced and both have remarried, which makes things difficult, though we do our level best to be even-handed between the two lots.

♥

Her family didn't want us to marry. They told us it would never last and they kept her bedroom ready, con-vinced it would all end and they would say 'We told you

*so'. But we've been together five years and what they
think doesn't bother us any more.*

♥

*On the eve of my wedding to my second wife, my mother
said to me, 'Are you absolutely sure about this?' It made
me furious.*

For worse, she says

*He refuses to go near some of my relations (in some cases
I can't blame him!) but I usually shame him into it.*

♥

*His parents have always resented me. They've never
really given me the time of day even after six years. He
tends to side with them over issues, which causes serious
conflicts. But he does help my family when they need a
hand.*

♥

*He stays out of the way when my family visits. He says
it's to give us family time together, but it seems like he's
avoiding them and I can tell it hurts their feelings.*

The Mother(-in-Law) of All Jokes

Why do mothers-in-law carry such a burden of ridicule?
Those of us who try to fulfil the role with affection and
in a generous spirit feel it's not deserved. But ambiva-
lence about this tricky relationship goes back a long time:

'While your mother-in-law is alive, domestic peace is out of the question,' wrote the Roman satirist, Juvenal, in the early second century. In the 20th century, the needle-sharp writer Edith Sitwell described Picasso as 'a delight-ful, kindly, friendly, simple little man. When I met him he was extremely excited and overjoyed because his mother-in-law had just died and he was looking forward to the funeral.'

Even not so very long ago, making fun of the mother-in-law was practically compulsory in a certain type of Brit-ish comedy. Les Dawson, the greatest specialist in mother-in-law jokes, wrote a book called *Hitler Was My Mother-in-Law*. You know the sort of thing: 'There was a knock at the door, I knew it was the mother-in-law because all the mice were throwing themselves on the traps.' In the TV series *The Fall and Rise of Reginald Perrin*, there was a recurrent vi-sual joke that my father used to find hilarious. Every time Reggie's wife said, 'my mother...' or Reggie said, 'your mother...' there was a split-second, almost subliminal shot of a hippopotamus trotting across the screen. Need-less to say my mother, who was built on generous lines, was not amused.

The convention of the mother-in-law joke has rath-er gone out of fashion, or at least has retreated to all-male gatherings in clubs or pubs. Nevertheless, the jokes are, in their way, reassuring. The placing of any difficulties inherent in a relationship at one remove from reality serves as a defence mechanism, and by mak-ing fun of a mutual antagonism that sometimes exists, one can neutralise it.

By contrast, specific problems between mothers-in-law and daughters-in-law are no laughing matter. In this most fraught of all family relationships, initial feelings of mutual suspicion are all too often confirmed. The chatrooms of mums' websites are clogged with rants about 'the MiL from hell' and mothers-in-law, for their part, complain about daughters-in-law who turn their sons against them or deny them access to their grandchildren. Some actually fear their daughters-in-law; others are merely nervous of them. What is going on?

Women don't get to choose their daughters-in-law, so it is natural if they are wary of each other at first. The one thing they have in common is that they love the same man – not usually a recipe for a harmonious relationship. The mother-in-law's thoughts (unexpressed, let's hope) are: 'I don't know what he sees in her' and 'She's not looking after him properly'. Meanwhile, the daughter-in-law is thinking, 'She wants him to stay Mummy's boy for ever' and 'Who does she think she is, telling me how to bring up my children?'

A daughter-in-law's hostility to her mother-in-law sometimes conceals a lack of confidence. With antennae poised to detect any hint of criticism, she interprets a kind offer to wash up the pots and pans as a slur on her housekeeping. The daughter-in-law whose house is always in a mess may, perhaps not very plausibly, blame her mother-in-law for not teaching her son to clean up after himself. The two most common complaints from daughters-in-law are: 'She interferes all the time' and 'She never offers to help out'.

For worse, he says

She finds my mother irritating but then, so do I.

♥

I don't feel she's ever given my mum a chance. She never stops moaning about her, although I can see Mum is really trying hard to please us.

♥

Her mum is a real bossy-boots, and I know she complains a lot about me behind my back. After a day with her my wife is completely knackered.

♥

My mother-in-law is a nagger and a whiner. She is divorced (no wonder) and on her own, so she makes prolonged visits to us. I know it's unhelpful of me, but I try to keep out of the way for fear of losing my temper.

For worse, she says

When she comes to stay she expects to be waited on hand and foot.

♥

My mother-in-law thinks I stole her youngest baby and I know, no matter how hard I try, it's never going to be good enough for her.

♥

She's a tricky customer. She probably resents having to go through me to get to her son and grandchildren – but I get along fine with my father-in-law.

♥

My first mother-in-law was a living nightmare, but we had a healthy respect for our mutual hatred. My father-in-law is lovely and we have stayed close even after we divorced.

♥

My mother and husband don't get on: they barely tolerate each other, so when she visits I am the mediator. Her presence puts him in one of his moods, and that gives her ammunition to criticise him. It's a vicious circle, and I do mean 'vicious'.

♥

He doesn't tell his mum off when she is out of order, and always takes her side against me.

♥

It's difficult to get it right but there are plenty of happy and affectionate relationships between mothers-in-law and daughters-in-law, where both sides have decided to make a go of it from the start. Sometimes it's helpful to listen to friends' complaints about the families they have married into but it's best not to make any assumptions: just because their relationship has turned sour, it doesn't mean yours will.

My advice is – don't assume your mother-in-law is jealous of you, ready to find fault with everything you do.

On the contrary, she's probably terrified of putting a foot wrong with you, and it's that which makes her seem cold. Give her the benefit of the doubt, and make the first move towards friendship.

If you find it hard going, start at a trivial level. There must be books or TV programmes you both enjoy, shops you both like, dishes you both cook. If you find nothing else in common, there's always your partner, so shoo him away and tell her how wonderful he is. You may not be interested in what he said when he fell off his bicycle at the age of four, or how much he still loves his mum's home-baked cookies, but if you suppress your yawns and ask her for the cookie recipe, you will be off to a good start.

If a relationship with the in-laws has been lukewarm, there will never be a better time to heal rifts than when a baby is born. One daughter-in-law said: 'I see myself as a portal through which my mother-in-law has to pass to see her grandchildren.' At last there is something in common, and there will never again be a dearth of conversational topics.

However, young mothers may require teeth-gritting forbearance to cope with the ecstatic new grandmother's well-meaning interference. Her advice, tips and presents may be unsolicited and not particularly welcome, but her motive is love. So make allowances: smile sweetly and listen to her advice, even if you don't intend to follow it. Accept all offers of practical help (free babysitters don't grow on trees) while making it clear, in the nicest way, that the baby's feeding and sleeping routines are not to be messed with. And no matter how hideous the hand-crocheted matinee jacket is, dress baby in it when Granny comes to visit.

For better, he says
My mother-in-law was a great influence on me. She and her family were high-minded and somehow everything that mine weren't.

♥

My partner loves my parents and enjoys staying with them, and they love her.

♥

I can't say we particularly like each other's mothers, but both are really happy that we love each other and look after each other and we get on all right when we see them.

♥

Although my mother could be very irritating, my wife was very good about inviting her to stay regularly, and put a lot of effort into making sure she had a fun weekend.

For better, she says
I like the way he makes a big fuss of my mother, and he calms her down when she's worried about her finances.

*No matter how hideous the hand-crocheted
matinee jacket is, dress baby in it when
Granny comes to visit.*

*My mother-in-law is great, we always have a real laugh
and seem to find the same things amusing about my
husband.*

♥

*I love my mother-in-law but she's in New Zealand. 'If you
ever split up, you're always welcome here,' she told me.*

♥

*My relationship with my in-laws is very important, and I
think of them as my parents too.*

♥

*When my mother comes over to see us, my husband makes
tea so I can have a good gossip with her, then he drives her
home.*

Tribal rituals
*Our relationship was marked by that habitual ex-
change of homespun nonsense, comically garbled
words, proposed imitations of supposed intona-
tions, and all those private jokes which are the
secret code of happy families.*

**Speak, Memory: an Autobiography Revisited,
Vladimir Nabokov (1951)**

As well as the secret code to which Nabokov refers,
each family has its own tribal rituals – its own way of

celebrating marriages, births and anniversaries. Even at the most trivial level, customs vary from one family to another. My husband and his siblings never fail to send each other birthday cards and ring each other up on the day, whereas my brother and I haven't acknowledged each other's birthdays for 50 years. It doesn't mean we're not devoted to each other.

Relationships with the in-laws are never more sorely tested than at Christmas. One family always puts a star at the top of the tree, and scorns the in-laws' custom of putting up a glittering angel. One lot puts mince pies out for Santa and roasts a goose for lunch; the other leaves carrots for Rudolph and does a turkey and all the trimmings for dinner.

Such differences are not worth discussing; none the less heated arguments do break out. The only way to handle them is to keep quiet and respect each household's traditions.

If one person's family isn't particularly sociable, but the other's relations really know how to party, the less social one may feel like a fish out of water at noisy, exuberant gatherings. The get-togethers may also reveal a side of a partner that isn't very attractive. But even if the whoopee cushion or Uncle Harold's blue jokes are excruciatingly embarrassing, it's best to grin and bear it, with the emphasis on 'grin'. Christmas only comes once a year, and weddings and landmark anniversaries even less frequently.

Just imagine how a gathering of a smaller, more introverted clan looks to the party animal: Aunt Gertrude sipping a thimbleful of dry sherry through pursed lips; a brother-in-law pontificating about the European Union? Nobody's family is perfect. As Desmond Tutu, the Nobel peace prizewinner, once said: 'You don't choose your family. They are God's gift to you, as you are to them.'

A DISASTER

I could not help wondering in my own
mind, as I contemplated the boiled leg of mutton
before me, previous to carving it, how it came to pass
that our joints of meat were of such extraordinary shapes –
and whether our butcher contracted for all the deformed sheep
that came into the world; but I kept my reflections to myself.

'My love,' said I to Dora, 'what have you got in that dish?'…

'Oysters, dear,' said Dora, timidly…' 'I bought a beautiful little barrel
of them, and the man said they were very good. But I – I am afraid
there's something the matter with them. They don't seem right.' Here
Dora shook her head, and diamonds twinkled in her eyes.

'They are only opened in both shells,' said I. 'Take the top one off, my love.'

'But it won't come off,' said Dora, trying very hard,
and looking very much distressed.

'Do you know, Copperfield,' said Traddles, cheerfully examining the
dish, 'I think it is in consequence – they are capital oysters, but I think
it is in consequence – of their never having been opened.'

They never had been opened; and we had no oyster-knives – and
couldn't have used them if we had; so we looked at the oysters and ate
the mutton. At least we ate as much of it as was done, and made up
with capers. If I had permitted him, I am satisfied that Traddles
would have made a perfect savage of himself, and eaten a plateful
of raw meat, to express enjoyment of the repast; but I would
hear of no such immolation on the altar of friendship, and
we had a course of bacon instead; there happening,
by good fortune, to be cold bacon in the larder.

David Copperfield,
Charles Dickens (1850)

5
BEST OF FRIENDS,
WORST OF FRIENDS

The most successful partnerships are outward-looking and inclusive. No relationship can thrive in a vacuum and, although in the early stages the couple has eyes only for each other and wants to spend every precious moment together, it's a mistake to depend entirely on each other for happiness. Couples who exclude outsiders soon become oversensitive to each other's faults. In the best relationships, a couple shares their happiness with friends as well as families. Sharing works both ways. The couple gives pleasure to family and friends, and benefits from the emotional and practical support received in return.

For better, he says
Over the years we've both stayed loyal to the friends we had before, as well as making new friends together.

Marriage has weeded out the less than special among our acquaintances and confirmed and strengthened the true friendships.

For better, she says

I moved from my native land to marry him, his friends were many and welcoming.

♥

We both meet new, mostly young, friends through our work.

♥

We're very lucky. We have very good friends who have lasted throughout our marriage.

♥

Perhaps I don't spend as much time with friends as I used to — even after 37 years I'd rather be with him.

The nice little couple

To dine with Mr and Mrs Chirrup is one of the pleasantest things in the world. Mr Chirrup has a bachelor friend, who lived with him in his own days of single blessedness, and to whom he is mightily attached. Contrary to the usual custom, this bachelor friend is no less a friend of Mrs

Chirrup's, and, consequently, whenever you dine with Mr and Mrs Chirrup, you meet the bachelor friend. It would put any reasonably-conditioned mortal into good-humour to observe the entire unanimity which subsists between these three; but there is a quiet welcome dimpling in Mrs Chirrup's face, a bustling hospitality oozing as it were out of the waistcoat-pockets of Mr Chirrup, and a patronising enjoyment of their cordiality and satisfaction on the part of the bachelor friend, which is quite delightful. On these occasions Mr Chirrup usually takes an opportunity of rallying the friend on being single, and the friend retorts on Mr Chirrup for being married, at which moments some single young ladies present are like to die of laughter; and we have more-than once observed them bestow looks upon the friend, which convinces us that his position is by no means a safe one, as, indeed, we hold no bachelor's to be who visits married friends and cracks jokes on wedlock, for certain it is that such men walk among traps and nets and pitfalls innumerable, and often find themselves down upon their knees at the altar rails, taking M or N for their wedded wives, before they know anything about the matter.

Sketches of Young Couples, Charles Dickens (1855)

———◆◆◆———

...let there be spaces in your togetherness
And let the winds of the heavens dance between you...

Fill each other's cup but drink not from one cup.
Give one another of your bread but eat not from
the same loaf.
Sing and dance together and be joyous, but let
each one of you be alone,
Even as the strings of a lute are alone though
they
quiver with the same music.

Give your hearts, but not into each other's keep-
ing.
For only the hand of Life can contain your hearts.
And stand together yet not too near together:
For the pillars of the temple stand apart,
And the oak tree and the cypress grow not in each
other's shadow.

The Prophet, Khalil Gibran (1923)

Many couples testify that, when they set up house together, it was particularly hard to adjust to the new constraints on their social lives. Evenings and week-ends would be taken up with wallpapering, painting, putting up shelves or shopping for a fridge-freezer. For her, the Bridget Jones days are over. It's goodbye to gig-gling over a bottle of Bulgarian red, and farewell to sobbing throughout a sentimental movie with her girl-friends. For him, there are fewer outings to the pub. Eve-nings spent slumped on the sofa with a takeaway, watching the big match with friends, become rare events.

Of course, from time to time, they have his mates or her girlfriends round for supper or Sunday lunch. Or one of them may entertain old friends while the other disappears. A wife says, 'When my friends come round, he vanishes to the bedroom to work on the computer, leaving us to talk girl's talk.' And a husband, 'If one of her old friends threatens to visit, I usually go fishing.'

I daresay it was good for me to be took such care of; but it cut me off from all my old friends something dreadful, ma'am: especially the women, ma'am. She never gave them a chance: she didn't indeed. She never understood that married people should take holidays from one another if they are to keep at all fresh. Not that I ever got tired of her, ma'am; but my! How I used to get tired of home life sometimes.

Getting Married, George Bernard Shaw (1908)

Everyone needs a respite from domestic life now and then and if your spouse finds it difficult to get on with any of your friends, seeing them separately on occasion may be the only way for you to stay in touch with them. No one should expect their other half to be overjoyed at the prospect of dinner with someone else's old work colleagues, listening to gossip about old times. The same applies to college reunions. By going our separate ways occasionally we can keep old friendships in good repair, knowing the best possible babysitter is at home. And if it's our turn to stay at home, we must try to be understanding about the hangover the next morning.

The morning after
MRS CHERRY OWEN

> Remember last night? In you reeled, my boy, as drunk as a deacon with a big wet bucket and a fish-frail full of stout and you looked at me and you said, 'God has come home!' you said, and then over the bucket you went, sprawling and bawling, and the floor was all flagons and eels.

CHERRY O

> Was I wounded?

MRS C.O.

> And then you took off your trousers   and   you   said, 'Does anybody want a fight!' Oh, you old baboon.

CHERRY O

> Give me a kiss.

MRS CO

> And then you sang 'Bread of Heaven', tenor and bass.

CHERRY O

> I always sing 'Bread of Heaven'.

MRS CO
> *And then you did a little dance on the table.*

CHERRY O
> *I did?*

MRS CO
> *Drop dead!*

CHERRY O
> *And then what did I do?*

MRS CO
> *Then you cried like a baby and said you were a poor drunk orphan with nowhere to go but the grave.*

CHERRY O
> *And what did I do next, my dear?*

MRS CO
> *Then you danced on the table all over again and said you were King Solomon Owen and I was your Mrs Sheba.*

CHERRY O
> *And then?*

MRS CO
> *And then I got you into bed and you snored all night like a brewery.*

(Mr and Mrs Cherry Owen laugh delightedly together)

Under Milk Wood, Dylan Thomas (1954)

The Pooters on the morning after

Carrie had commenced her breakfast when I entered the parlour. I helped myself to a cup of tea, and I said, perfectly calmly and quietly: 'Carrie, I wish a little explanation of your conduct last night.'

She replied, 'Indeed! And I desire something more than a little explanation of your conduct the night before.'

I said, coolly: 'Really, I don't understand you.' Carrie said sneeringly: 'Probably not; you were scarcely in a condition to understand anything.'

I was astounded at this insinuation and simply ejaculated: 'Caroline!'

She said: 'Don't be theatrical, it has no effect on me. Reserve that tone for your new friend, Mister Farmerson, the ironmonger.' Etc. etc.

Diary of a Nobody, George and Weedon Grossmith (1892)

However generous and understanding our spouses are about letting us out on our own, though, it is a sad but inevitable fact that, after marriage, we grow away from some of our former friends. Lives take different directions and there will be less in common as time goes by. Before marriage, life is mostly about hanging out with other single people but, after setting up house together, couples often gravitate towards other couples with whom they suddenly have a great deal in common. Instead of having a group of 'her' friends and a group of 'his', they make mutual friends. Conversations about house prices and school catchment areas that might formerly have had them looking surreptitiously at their watches suddenly become fascinating topics; they find themselves happy to discuss whether eco-friendly washing products really get shirts clean, and whether to get a puppy for the baby's sake, or have a baby for the puppy's sake. Their new friends may be people with whom, formerly, they may not have had much in common, but who, since the arrival of children, have become the crux of their social life.

When Children Arrive

He says
The arrival of children has changed things. It means we see much less of those friends who don't have children.

♥

We moved to a new area, leaving friends behind, but my partner has made new friends through being pregnant.

♥

Her friends without children have been very understanding about her not being able to go out as much as she used to. They come to us instead.

She says
It's having kids rather than marriage in itself that affects

friendships. I'm so tired all the time, and journeys to visit friends at a distance just seem too much.

♥

I go out of my way to keep in touch with my girlfriends from before we got married. The other day two of them came to see the new baby and my partner cooked us all lunch and made drinks and was the perfect husband.

⁂

RULE ONE: Neither party to a sacred union should run down, disparage or badmouth the other's former girls or beaux, as the case may be. The tendency to attack the character, looks, intelligence, capability, and achievements of one's mate's friends of the opposite sex is a common cause of domestic discontent. Sweetheart-slurring, as we will call this deplorable practice, is encouraged by a long spell of gloomy weather, too many highballs, hangovers, and the suspicion that one's spouse is hiding, and finding, letters in a hollow tree...

Aspersions, insinuations, reflections or just plain cracks about old boy friends and girl friends should be avoided at all times. Here are some of the expressions that should be especially eschewed: 'That waffle-fingered, minor-league third baseman you latched on to at Cornell'; 'You know the girl I mean — the one with the hips who couldn't read'; 'That old flame of yours with the vocabu-

lary of a hoot owl'; and 'You remember her — that old bat who chewed gum and dressed like Daniel Boone'.

This kind of derogatory remark, if persisted in by one or both parties to a marriage, will surely lead to divorce or, at best, a blow on the head with a glass ashtray.

My Own Ten Rules for a Happy Marriage, James Thurber (1953)

Inevitably, too, when a friend marries someone we dislike, or consider unworthy, that friendship suffers. The fact that we do not care for a friend's husband (or wife) is very difficult to hide, and can quickly create no-go areas in a relationship that was formerly easy and relaxed. In *Pride and Prejudice*, Jane Austen describes how Elizabeth Bennet felt when her friend Charlotte married the ghastly Mr Collins, whom Elizabeth herself had turned down. 'When Mr Collins said any thing of which his wife might reasonably be ashamed, which certainly was not unseldom, she [Elizabeth] involuntarily turned her eye on Charlotte. Once or twice she could discern a faint blush; but in general Charlotte wisely did not hear.' The friendship between Elizabeth and Charlotte continued, but with a reserve that hadn't existed before.

And then there is the tricky area of friend 'ownership'.

Married couples can be outrageously proprietorial of old friends – particularly of men who have reached a certain age, either still single, or divorced or widowed. 'By the time you are 39 your friends have taken possession of you,' the author Julian Fellowes explains. 'You are not just a bachelor. You are their bachelor.' Married couples cherish their 'spare man'. They pet him and spoil him and are disappointed when he can no longer be invited without his girlfriend. They may even feel like cold-shouldering the new woman in his life. But if they are true friends, it won't take them long to warm to her and make her welcome.

Home Truths

> *There is nothing I enjoy more than noisy, marital disharmony at a dinner party. It lifts the evening in a way no menu or cabaret can.*
>
> **Julian Fellowes**

It might be pasta and salad with copious plonk or herb-stuffed courgette flowers followed by baked sea bass with lavender and honey parfait for pudding and a different vintage wine with each course. Whatever the menu, one of the great pleasures of domestic life is entertaining friends. Or at least, it should be. But the atmosphere can sometimes be as tense as a strung bow, and it doesn't go unnoticed by the guests.

For a start, it's a bad hair day – too much time was spent peeling prawns and carving radishes into roses so there was no time for a shampoo and blow-dry. Just when the table was laid, the cat leapt up and left a trail of paw marks over the pristine tablecloth. The crème brulée curdled.

Now, it seems you used up all the hot water trying to clean a burnt saucepan, and there isn't enough left for a quick bath. Just as you are wondering how long it will take for the immersion heater to kick in, the man of the house breezes in and puts a box of wine bottles on the worktop where some parsley was about to be chopped. 'Have you tidied the sitting room?' he says. He goes to the cooker and lifts the lid off a simmering casserole. 'Gosh, what's this? Smells a bit insipid. Have you tasted it? Shall we try adding some curry powder?'

And the guests don't help. One couple arrives having had the usual row on their journey. Is that a scowl or a hastily assembled grin? Another pair have been to a drinks party and can hardly stand upright, and the third have just phoned to say their Sat Nav has taken them halfway to Burton-on-Trent instead of Bourton-on-the-Water.

In real life these minor disasters never happen all at once, but they have all been known to happen. Not to mention the telephone ringing as the meat is coming out of the oven. It's a guest asking, 'Did I tell you we're veg-

'*Did I tell you we're vegetarian?*'

etarian?' Answering them means the beef will never be medium-rare: not that they would care. Then the home-grown broad beans are somehow overcooked (in our marriage this is the worst culinary crime).

To expect a sense of humour at such times is asking a bit much, but a sense of proportion is sorely needed. After all, it's only the hosts who are distressed by the mishaps. Guests will be happy as long as their glasses are kept filled and the company is congenial.

A success
Mrs Bennet: 'I think everything has passed off uncommonly well, I assure you. The dinner was as well dressed as any I ever saw. The venison was roasted to a turn — and everybody said, they never saw so fat a haunch. The soup was fifty times better than what we had at the Lucas's last week; and even Mr Darcy acknowledged that the partridges were remarkably well done; and I suppose he has two or three French cooks at least.'
Pride and Prejudice, Jane Austen (1813)

In vino veritas — especially when it is *veritas domestica* — should be translated as 'home truths', preferably delivered in front of an audience of friends. Every couple will be guilty of playing to the gallery in this way at some point in their relationship. But remember there are nice ways to tease a partner when among friends – as one wife put it, 'Even when he's having a go at me, he makes me laugh; he's so good at observing my and other people's behaviour and recounting it in a really funny way, so it's impossible to take offence' – and there are downright nasty ways. If bantering altercation descends to straight abuse, the audience feels uncomfortable.

Playing bridge once, I heard a husband call his wife a 'stupid bitch'. She blithely ignored it, being, I suppose, accustomed to his ways. Everyone else in the room may have sympathised with his feelings when she trumped his ace, but we couldn't help but feel shocked and unhappy at the way he expressed them.

RULE THREE: A husband should not insult his wife publicly, at parties. He should insult her in the privacy of the home. Thus, if a man thinks the soufflés his wife makes are as tough as an out-fielder's glove, he should tell her so when they are at home, not when they are out at a formal dinner party where a perfect soufflé has just been served. The same rule applies to the wife. She should not regale his men friends, or women friends, with hilarious accounts of her husband's clumsiness, remarking that he dances like

a 1907 Pope Hartford, or that he locked himself in the children's rabbit pen and couldn't get out. All parties must end finally, and the husband or wife who has revealed all may find that there is hell to pay in the taxi going home.

My Own Ten Rules for a Happy Marriage, James Thurber (1953)

Giving Away the Punchline, and Other Crimes

The man who says his wife can't take a joke, forgets that she took him.'
Oscar Wilde (1854-1900)

A sense of humour is a highly valued attribute in a spouse. One husband says, 'When we're on our own, she makes witty observations about people and events around us. In a group, she's amusing and friendly and tells a good story, usually against herself.'

And another says of his wife, 'She makes people laugh.' Women, too, appreciate a talent to amuse: 'My husband's sense of humour is one of his best features,' says one, with pride. 'He's brilliant at telling stories – inevitably, after 15 years together, the jokes are familiar, but I don't mind how often I hear them.'

Mr Pooter makes a joke

April 27 [Mr Pooter's friend Cummings calls, to leave the *Bicycle News*.] *Another ring at the bell; it was Gowing... I said: 'A very extraordinary thing has struck me.' 'Something funny, as usual,' said Cummings. 'Yes,' I replied, 'I think even you will say so this time. It's concerning you both; for doesn't it seem odd that Gowing's always coming and Cummings' always going?' Carrie* [Mrs Pooter]... *went into fits of laughter, and as for myself, I fairly doubled up in my chair, till it cracked beneath me. I think this was one of the best jokes I have ever made.*

Then imagine my astonishment on perceiving both Cummings and Gowing perfectly silent, and without a smile on their faces.

Diary of a Nobody, George and Weedon Grossmith (1892)

But it's not always a case of mutual admiration when it comes to telling anecdotes. When one partner holds the floor, much can be revealed about their relationship by the reactions of the other partner.

Whenever Odette told a stupid story, Swann listened to his wife with a compliance, a gaiety, almost an admiration where some remnants of sensuousness must have played a part; on the other hand, in the same conversation, whatever he would say that was refined, or even profound, was usually received by Odette without interest, quickly, impatiently and was sometimes contradicted with severity. And one might conclude that this enslavement of the elite to vulgarity was the rule in many households...

Remembrance of Things Past: volume II, Marcel Proust (1913)

If only we could all be less like Odette and more like Swann, or like the husband whose wife says, 'He always lets me finish my jokes and laughs the loudest.' Alas, familiarity with a spouse's party pieces too often breeds contempt, and jokes, however funny, can be conversation stoppers. If a partner is a teller of jokes, be ready to fill the silence that follows 'the one about...' after the initial guffaw. And we should curb our impulse to argue in public over the details of a story, and resist the temptation to interrupt. Waiting our turn, and allowing trivial mistakes to go uncorrected does oil the conversational wheels.

For worse, she says
He takes himself far too seriously and when he can

find anyone to listen, tells long and boring stories,
facts about the war, and such like.

♥

Like most husbands, he tells the same old jokes again and
again, till I could scream. And I'm not the only one that's
heard them before.

♥

When we have people to lunch in the summer, he cooks
a few sausages and burgers on the barbeque. I've done
all the salads, potatoes, set the table, washed up etc, but
suddenly he's Jamie Oliver: 'There's nothing to this
cooking lark!'

♥

He drinks too much when we're out with our mates, laughs
loudly at non-funny things and gets gabby and louder
than normal.

♥

He signals to me to leave and I say farewells, then he
spends another 20 minutes (always exactly, I've timed it)
so it looks as if I'm hurrying him away against his will.

♥

If we have friends to dinner, just at the point I'm really
tired and hoping they will leave soon, he opens another
bottle and fills everybody's glasses.

For worse, he says
She talks too much — tales of her dashing younger days
are repeated ad nauseam.

♥

Her stories sometimes go into unnecessary detail, like Ronnie Corbett's 'nested' stories, but not so funny. She gets in a muddle so the punchline never materialises.

♥

She's terribly indiscreet and blabs about intimate and personal things I'd rather she kept quiet about.

♥

Like most women she's hopeless at telling jokes and, because she has no concept of a punchline, she often ruins mine!

♥

The difference between us is that she likes meeting people and I only like meeting certain people. If we're asked out, she accepts with alacrity, whereas I might say, 'Oh, the So-and-sos, aren't they a bit heavy?' Having said that, I have sometimes been out under duress and quite enjoyed myself.

♥

It's a mystery how she can take so long getting ready to go out. Every time we have to go through a litany of 'Does this top go with the skirt? Shall I wear these shoes or those? Do I look better with or without the belt?'

♥

She tells me off in front of our friends for drinking too much.

For better, he says

When we go out to dinner with friends, we enjoy talking about it afterwards and we usually agree about the ghastliness or niceness of fellow guests.

♥

We share secret jokes and often catch each other's eye across the table.

♥

She is very, very loyal in all things.

For better, she says

He's a wonderful, very generous host, loves entertaining and always makes sure everyone has a lovely time.

♥

I sometimes overhear him saying nice things about me and it gives me such a thrill.

♥

We love going home after spending an evening with friends, just happy to be together.

Keeping Friendships in Good Repair – some Dos and Don'ts

Do try and stay in touch with friends. It may be a logistical nightmare but it is worth it in the long run. If you are inclined to be a bit of a hermit, make an effort to be more sociable.

Don't slag off a partner to friends, however wittily. Between affectionate teasing and unkind sarcasm there's a line that shouldn't be crossed.

Don't bang on to a wife about how young her old school-friend looks, how an old girlfriend has kept her figure or what a brilliant cook her cousin's wife is.

Don't bang on to a husband about what a fine head of hair his old friend still has, how fit he is, how rich he has become, and what great holidays he takes his wife on.

Do, even with close friends, observe the boundary between delicious gossip and prurient indiscretion about your own and other people's private lives.

Don't grudge a partner going off to watch or play sport. If you feel jealous of his companions, encourage him to bring them home so you can get to know them. Or, if you'd rather not, just be glad of the extra time to yourself.

Don't insist on a party post-mortem. If one of you got drunk, snogged on the dance floor or otherwise 'made a fool of yourself', keep quiet. Recriminations are pointless.

While waiting for her to finish her make-up, make just one more call, feed the dog, change her mind about the restaurant, get out of the bath, go online to check her email, do something about her hair... do not sit in the car with the engine running, the music turned up excessively loud, screeching in frustration at the top of your lungs. You know you aren't going anywhere till she's good and ready and so does she. Just wait.

Eric Idle in the Daily Telegraph

Life has taught us that love does not consist in gazing at each other. But in looking outward together in the same direction

Antoine de Saint Exupéry (1900-1944)

MONEY (THAT'S WHAT I WANT)

The best things in life are free
But you can keep 'em for the birds and bees;
Now give me money, (that's what I want) that's what I want,
(That's what I want) That's what I want (That's what I want) yeah,
That's what I want.

Your lovin' gives me such a thrill,
But your lovin' don't pay my bills;

Money don't get everything it's true,
What it don't get I can't use;

Well, now give me money, (That's what I want)
A lotta money, (That's what I want)
Oh yeah, I wanna be free, (That's what I want)
Oh, lotta money, (That's what I want)
That's what I want (That's what I want) yeah,
That's what I want.

Well, now give me money, (That's what I want)
A lotta money, (That's what I want)
Wo, yeah, you need money (That's what I want)
Gimme money, (That's what I want)
That's what I want (That's what I want)
That's what I want.

Barrett Strong (1959)

6

FOR RICHER FOR POORER

A wife is often quite sensible. A little love from her husband can make her smile. But most wifes [sic] have lot of desires. This is the root cause of all quarrels. A wife need to understand what is the salary or income of his husband and accordingly she should demand anything from her husband. A wife don't understand how difficult it is to make money in business or doing some job. A husband feels irritating when his wife ask for more and more money. Its easy to spend money but very difficult to earn money. If a wife understand this and restrict her desires, the life could go in a much better way.

As posted on an internet chatroom

In some cultures marriage is still very much a business transaction. Brides bring dowries to the partnership and are paid for with cows, goats, gold or stock market investments: husband and wife each contribute to the domestic economy in their different ways.

Nowadays, in the west, few women would admit to being 'material girls' when it comes to choosing a husband. Yet there does seem to be an instinct quite independent of love that drives people towards the domestic security of marriage. The urge may be triggered by the ticking of the biological clock, encouraged by happily married friends and increased by parental pressure. Whatever the complex combination of motives, it reflects a practical view of marriage.

Three views of a marriage of convenience:

[Charlotte] 'I am not romantic you know. I never was. I ask only for a comfortable home; and considering Mr Collins's character, connections, and situation in life, I am convinced that my chance of happiness with him is as fair as most people can boast on entering the marriage state.'

[Darcy] 'Mr Collins appears very fortunate in his choice of a wife.'

[Elizabeth] 'Yes, indeed; his friends may well rejoice in his having met with one of the few sensible women who would have accepted him, or have

made him happy if they had. My friend has an excellent understanding — though I am not certain that I consider her marrying Mr Collins as the wisest thing she ever did. She seems perfectly happy, however, and in a prudential light, it is certainly a very good match for her.'

Pride and Prejudice, Jane Austen (1813)

Setting up house together, even in one or two small rooms, is no mean feat and inevitably involves financial commitment. Rent must be paid or a mortgage serviced and for many couples the financial burden is heavy. Humphrey Repton, at the end of the 18th century, declared, 'A cottage is a dwelling where happiness may reside unsupported by wealth', but these days a thatched-roof cottage with roses and honeysuckle round the door doesn't come cheap. Even a poetic 'artist's garret', known today less romantically and more expensively as a penthouse or loft conversion, is beyond the means of average newly-weds.

Perhaps the best way for an impoverished couple to get a toehold on the property ladder is by spotting the next up-and-coming bohemian quarter. Some 40 years ago we thought we had achieved this with our first house in Notting Hill in London, acquired with a millstone of a mortgage. It was a run-down neighbourhood in those days, but, sure enough, it finally upped and came. But not, alas, until five years after we had sold the house and moved on.

—————————•———✦◦✦———•—————————

Neither a borrower nor a lender be;
For loan oft loses both itself and friend,
And borrowing dulls the edge of husbandry.
**Polonius in *Hamlet*, William Shake-
speare (1603)**

—————————•———✦◦✦———•—————————

When a couple become homeowners, other ambitions follow, all with financial implications: a second car, a dream kitchen, a plasma screen, a loft extension, and a brace of babies, sometimes in that order of priority. Once on the financial treadmill, there's no getting off. It's the same for everyone, and money troubles all too often cast a shadow over a couple's happiness.

It's a sad fact that, according to Relate, money is at the root of most marriage breakdowns. Yet many financial problems can be anticipated and avoided. My father was fond of saying 'You must cut your coat according to your cloth'. Impeccable advice, if a little dreary. I pictured myself laying out a paper pattern on top of material that was a few inches too narrow, so that I would end up looking like Beatrix Potter's Tom Kitten in his little blue coat, bursting at the seams, with every button straining to its limit.

When it comes to money, we can take our pick of clichés: 'The best things in life are free,' and 'The love of money is the root of all evil' will do nicely for the un-

The best way for an impoverished couple to get a toehold on the property ladder is by spotting the next up-and-coming bohemian quarter...

worldly. Big spenders might prefer to point out that you can't take it with you and sing with the 19th-century poet Arthur Hugh Clough, 'How pleasant it is to have money, heigh-ho! How pleasant it is to have money'. But the vast majority of sayings about money are, rather depressingly, in praise of thrift: 'A fool and his money are soon parted'; 'Look after the pennies and the pounds will look after themselves'; 'Beggars can't be choosers'.

In the early days of their marriage, George and Martha Washington were not well off, but Martha's attitude was positive: 'I am determined,' she wrote, 'to be cheerful and happy in whatever situation I may be… the greater part of our happiness or misary [sic] depends on our dispositions, and not on our circumstances.'

Usually money or the lack of it only disrupts married life when attitudes are at variance, or when comparison with the lifestyle of other couples gives rise to envy and discontent. Take the Haves and Have-Notts. The two couples have known each other since their student days, but their paths have diverged. Richard and Imogen Have are hugely prosperous, owing to successful careers in the world of IT, whilst John and Janet Have-Nott find life a bit of a struggle on his teacher's salary.

Richard and Imo have invited Janet and John to lunch. The Have-Notts arrive in their seen-better-days family hatchback and park it between Richard's four-wheel drive and Imo's sporty two-seater. The children tumble out and disappear with their hosts' kids in a flurry of kicked-up gravel. They will be neither seen nor heard until lunch because there is a trampoline, climbing frame, swing, go-cart and other delights to keep them occupied.

The adults go on to the terrace and Richard opens a bottle of champagne: not to celebrate anything in particular, it's just good to see old friends. Janet admires the garden. 'We're so lucky,' says Imo. 'I can't tell a weed from a rose. Adam, our gardener, does it all. He's worth his weight in gold.' Janet, who's been weeding her allotment all morning, sits on her hands to hide her grimy, broken fingernails. Richard is tipping John off about the next good thing on the stock market, unaware that his old friend doesn't have the wherewithal to invest. Imo goes on to complain about the parking problem when she goes to London to shop in the sales — it's the designer shops, she says, that have the real bargains.

By the time the Haves finish talking about which are the best private schools and whether to go skiing or to Barbados for their winter holidays, the H-Ns are bored as well as envious. And on the way home they can't help feeling a little dissatisfied with each other. Janet wishes John was not in such a dead-end job. Why can't he be more of a whiz-kid, like Richard? John thinks it's time he had another go at Janet about going back to work full-time. The extra income would make all the difference.

However, their marriage is rock solid, so, by the time they get home, their good humour is restored, and when the Haves make a return visit a few months later, it's Richard and Imo's turn to feel a frisson of envy. Their less well-off friends take so much pleasure in conjuring an aromatic stew out of a cheap cut of meat, and so much pride in the baby carrots and beans they have grown themselves. After lunch they all go to the park to feed the ducks and play football, which the Have children consider a great adventure.

Poverty is relative; we can all point to someone better off than we are, and it's not surprising if we occasionally envy them. When things are not going well, it's tempting to think they would go better if we were richer, and to compare a partner unfavourably with someone whose material success has been greater. But when Janet Have-Nott falls prey to such thoughts, she wouldn't dream of undermining her husband's confidence by making the comparisons out loud.

Katharine Whitehorn's rule, 'not to talk about money with people who have much more or much less than you', is spot-on.

Getting It and Spending It

In the days before everyone had a bank account, the working man got his wage packet on a Friday. Depending on his character and inclination, he would either hand the money over to his wife and she would give him his beer money and put the rest in the teapot for safety, or else he would give her as much 'housekeeping' as he thought fit and take the rest to the pub. Or, worst of all, he might visit the pub on his way home and his wife would never see his wages at all.

In middle-class households, things were not very different. Sometimes the husband paid an allowance to his wife to cover all her personal needs as well as the household expenses. In other families, the wife might receive a 'dress allowance' in addition to housekeeping money. In either case, if the husband was unduly thrifty (let's call him downright mean), his wife might have to beseech him to fork out every time she needed a dress or shoes.

Mr Pooter is promoted

Mr Perkupp said: '…there will be a considerable increase in your salary, which, it is quite unnecessary for me to say, you fully deserve. I have an appointment at two; but you shall hear more tomorrow.'

He then left the room quickly, and I was not even allowed time or thought to express a single word of grateful thanks to him. I need not say how dear Carrie received this joyful news. With perfect simplicity she said: 'At last we shall be able to have a chimney-glass for the back drawing-room, which we always wanted.' I added: 'Yes, and at last you shall have that little costume which you saw at Peter Robinson's so cheap.'

Diary of a Nobody, George and Weedon Grossmith (1892)

Women remained at the mercy of their husbands' generosity until the early 20th century. Although in the marriage service, besides 'for richer, for poorer' the words 'with all my worldly goods I thee endow' were spoken by the bridegroom, in most marriages that vow was consistently broken. The true situation would be more accurately expressed by the phrase. 'What's yours is mine, and what's mine's my own'. Certainly that was the general legal view of a married woman's property, and many women stayed in unhappy marriages for fear of becoming destitute.

Nowadays the norm is for both partners to earn, and the customary promise is 'All my wordly goods with thee I share'. Nevertheless, a joint bank account is not necessarily a good idea. Although it enables a couple to be open about their expenditure, and have no secrets from each other, the arrival of the bank statement can be a dangerous flashpoint.

On examining it, each partner inevitably feels the other has been more extravagant or spent less wisely, and feels aggrieved. The best arrangement is probably for each person to have their own bank account and for them to have a joint account for household spending, into which they both pay an agreed amount in proportion with their income.

When they tried to stop me spending all my pocket

[174]

*money at once, because there'd be none left, I said:
'But I don't want any left, I just want lots and lots
of toys' — not an attitude to endear one eventually
to a cautious spouse.*

Selective Memory, **Katharine Whitehorn
(2007)**

———————◆◆◆◆◆———————

One person's extravagance is another's necessity. A
three-year-old says 'but I need an icecream'. He truly believes it. His father, a keen golfer, truly believes he needs a
new driver, as used by Tiger Woods. His friends will never
play golf with him again, he thinks, unless he ups his game
by making the investment. His wife needs a pair of green
patent leather shoes to wear with her black dress and a
black suede pair to wear with her red suit. What's more,
she knows she could have both for the price of the Tiger
Woods driver. She tells her husband so. 'I simply don't
understand it,' she says. 'You've got two drivers already,
or is it three? How many can you play with at once, for
God's sake?' 'You're the one who doesn't understand,' he
counters. 'How can you grudge me this? Golf is my one
way of relaxing after a week of hard graft. You've got cupboards full of shoes already. You're Imelda Marcos. There
must be shoes in there you haven't worn for three years.
Why don't you give them an outing instead of buying new
ones?' And so it goes on.

Too much criticism of a partner's spending may drive it
underground, which is never a good thing.

The confessions of a catalogue addict
*I developed a system of intercepting the postman
and hiding the evidence of my mistakes. Several
pairs of shoes, too tight and too difficult to parcel up
and send back, lurked at the back of the cupboard,
and hungry moths slowly unravelled a half-price
cashmere cardigan, while I waited in vain to get
down to size 10. I suffered increasingly unpleasant
sensations of guilt — not just about wasting money
but also about my sly and furtive behaviour. Now
I've more or less kicked the habit but, as with other
addictions, you're never completely cured. Since
I owned up to my partner, he's helped me resist
temptation, and when I do occasionally succumb,
it's become an affectionate joke between us.*
Internet chatroom

Different attitudes to money, which can cause so much
friction, can often be traced back to each partner's up-
bringing. Children whose parents were always saving for a
rainy day and said things like 'We can't afford it' and 'You
must think I'm made of money' sometimes rebel in later
life. Their attitude to spending becomes 'I want it now. I
don't care how much it costs, I deserve a treat.' On the
other hand, the children of parents who are feckless about
money may end up with a terror of getting into debt.

Mr Bennet had very often wished, before this period of his life, that, instead of spending his whole income, he had laid by an annual sum, for the better provision of his children, and of his wife, if she survived him. He now wished it more than ever. Had he done his duty in that respect, Lydia need not have been indebted to her uncle, for whatever of honour or credit could not be purchased for her. The satisfaction of prevailing on one of the most worthless young men in Great Britain to be her husband, might then have rested in its proper place.

Pride and Prejudice, Jane Austen (1813)

For better, he says

She's happy to encourage my whims, and doesn't mind me spending on my cameras, books etc.

♥

She's very unselfish, I have to talk her into spending money on herself.

For better, she says

If we've got the money to spare, I can have anything I want within reason!

♥

We usually see eye to eye about the big items of expenditure; it's the little niggly extravagances we argue about.

♥

He's generous to a fault.

For worse, he says
She's very impulsive and, like all women, she can't resist a bargain.

♥

She likes labels — because of this she doesn't always get the quality / value balance right.

♥

I've tried to teach her how to read a balance sheet but she doesn't seem able to grasp it.

♥

She complains I'm extravagant when I buy decent wine; she doesn't understand that I like to be generous to our friends.

For worse, she says
He always buys designer labels. To me they seem expensive and pointless.

♥

He takes taxis everywhere; he won't go by bus or tube.

♥

He's not exactly mean, but very careful with money: too much so actually.

♥

♥

He runs up huge bills on his credit cards.

When Money's Too Tight to Mention...

My father, when tackling me, more in sorrow than in anger, about my youthful overdraft, would quote Mr Micawber in *David Copperfield*: 'Annual income twenty pounds, annual expenditure nineteen nineteen six, result happiness. Annual income twenty pounds, annual expenditure twenty pounds nought and six, result misery.'

How lucky for Mr Micawber that credit cards hadn't been invented. If they had, the difference between happiness and misery might have been not pence, but pounds, and hundreds of them, if not thousands. In our 'live now, pay later' culture, it's only too easy to get into debt. It may be possible to recycle debts from one credit card to another so that the buck never stops, but the debt itself just grows and grows, and the worry that goes with it is destructive of family life.

'Really I think you should explain some of these.' [Lord Rule] drew the sheaf of bills out of his pocket and gave them to [his wife].

On the top lay a sheet of paper covered with Mr Gisborne's neat figures. Horatia gazed in dismay at the alarming total. 'Are they — all mine?' she faltered.

'All yours,' said his lordship calmly.

Horatia swallowed. 'I d-didn't mean to spend as m-much as that. Indeed I c-can't imagine how it can have come about.'

The Earl took the bills from her, and began to turn them over. 'No,' he agreed, 'I have often thought it very odd how bills mount up. And one must dress, after all.'

'Yes,' nodded Horatia, more hopefully. 'You do understand that, d-don't you, Marcus?'

'Perfectly. But — forgive my curiosity, Horry — do you invariably pay a hundred and twenty guineas for a pair of shoes?'

'What?' shrieked Horatia. The Earl showed her the bill. She stared at it with dawning consternation. 'Oh!' she said. 'I — I remember now. You see, Marcus, they — they have heels studded with emeralds.'

The Convenient Marriage, Georgette Heyer (1934)

Once in debt, how do you get out? One friend thought she knew the answer. Having been brought up by prosperous parents in a sheltered environment, she had never had to worry about financial matters in her youth, and when her husband, struggling to make ends meet, admitted his overdraft had spiralled out of control, she is reputed to have said brightly, in an effort to be helpful, 'Why don't you sell some shares?'

If only it were that simple. The best advice I can offer is, don't blame one another, cut back and stop borrowing and, if it is possible to find a living, breathing bank manager, as opposed to one who only exists inside a computer, go together and talk through the problems. The key thing is not to let your mutual worry about money become a source of mutual recrimination.

[Mr Bennet] turned to his daughter and said,

'Jane, I congratulate you. You will be a very happy woman.'

Jane went to him instantly, kissed him, and thanked him for his goodness.

'You are a good girl,' he replied, 'and I have great pleasure in thinking you will be so happily settled. I have not a doubt of your doing very well together. Your tempers are by no means unlike. You are each of you so complying, that nothing will ever be resolved on; so easy, that every servant will cheat you, and so generous, that you will always exceed your income.'

'I hope not so. Imprudence or thoughtlessness in money matters would be unpardonable in me.'

'Exceed their income! My dear Mr Bennet,' cried his wife, 'what are you talking of? Why, he

has four or five thousand a-year, and very likely more.'

Pride and Prejudice, Jane Austen (1813)

A Running-away Fund

The idea of a separate nest egg may seem a strange ingredient in the recipe for an open and happy marriage, but it's a system that comes highly recommended: 'I call it my running-away money,' says a friend, '…not that I have any intention of running away — we are as happy as can be — but I like to know it's there if I ever need it. You may keep joint or separate bank accounts, or both, and you may, as a couple, be wonderfully prudent about building up savings and pension funds for your old age, but you will still find it reassuring to have some money of your own. It needn't be a large amount but it should be inviolable. Even if you have a financial crisis and your partner comes begging you for it on bended knee, you must refuse. The point is, it symbolises your independence, and even if you feel you are joined at the hip, you still need that. Besides, you'd be surprised how much interest it earns.'

THE MERCHANT'S TALE

Well may the sick man wail and even weep
Who has no wife the house to clean and keep.
I warn you now, if wisely you would work,
Love well your wife, as Jesus loves His Kirk.
For if you love yourself, you love your wife;
No man hates his own flesh, but through his life
He fosters it, and so I bid you strive
To cherish her, or you shall never thrive.

Husband and wife, despite men's jape or play,
Of all the world's folk hold the safest way;
They are so knit there may no harm betide.
Especially upon the good wife's side.
For which this January, of whom I told,
Did well consider, in his days grown old.
The pleasant life, the virtuous rest complete
That are in marriage, always honey-sweet;
And for his friends upon a day he sent
To tell them the effect of his intent.

The Canterbury Tales, Geoffrey Chaucer
(c. 1343-1400)

7

IN SICKNESS AND IN HEALTH

*When pain and anguish wring the brow, a
ministering angel thou.*
Sir Walter Scott (1771-1832)

When someone we love is ill, it can be a difficult and
anxious time. Whether we have a natural talent for nursing
or are as clumsy in the sickroom as a bull in a china shop,
caring is an emotional experience, and the combination of
worry and wakeful nights is tiring. Fatigue may make us
short with the patient, with children and with anyone else
who happens to be around, and guilt will then be added
to the burden. The 'nurse' who manages to remain sympathetic, with never a cross word throughout a partner's
illness, deserves a medal.

We all handle illness differently, of course – the general
consensus being that a man with a snuffle acts as if he

were at death's door, whereas a woman, even when she is at death's door, will soldier on, never complaining. As the saying goes, 'Kids get colds, men get flu, women get on with it'.

My husband took himself off to bed early one evening with a headache. At 3 am he woke me, convinced he had meningitis, and asked me to call the doctor. I thought he was fussing unnecessarily, so I pointed out that one of the symptoms of meningitis is aversion to light, and it hadn't bothered him while playing on the computer all evening. He squinted at the bedside light and said, in a weak and croaky voice, that he thought it did hurt his eyes. I told him a stiff neck was another symptom. He moved his head slowly back from looking at the light. 'Yes, my neck is a bit stiff.' I kept refusing to make the call, and eventually he rang the emergency doctor himself and called him out. The doctor diagnosed... a headache.

Internet chatroom

Another husband is, according to his wife, not only a hypochondriac, but also a hoaxer, attention seeker, drama queen and baby. Once, when he complained of a chest pain, she gave in to his piteous pleas and drove him to the doctor. 'His act was unbelievable – he could have got a scholarship to RADA. The doctor asked him if he thought he was dying, and sent him to the nurse for an ECG. There was nothing wrong with him and the minute we got home he said he was starving and what about a fry-up?'

The question 'How are you?' has only two acceptable answers: 'Very well, thank you' and 'Good, thanks'. If, when we enquire, we get the answer 'Mustn't grumble', we can be fairly sure someone is about to do just that. If the answer is: 'I don't seem to be able to shake off this cold' or 'My sinuses are playing up again', we are definitely in the presence of a hypochondriac and he is about to enjoy bad health by sharing the gory details.

Forgive me if I keep referring to 'he'. Of course, hypochondria is found in women as well as men. The person who, at the first sign of a sniffle or a snuffle, demands a thermometer, can be of either sex. The new-fangled gadget we stick in the ear won't do for my own favourite sufferer. For him it must be an old-fashioned glass rod with mercury inside. If the mercury creeps above normal he either retires to bed, turns his face to the wall and groans, or drags himself, a halo of virtuous self-pity hovering around his poor sick head, to work. It's strange how a man with a feverish and infectious cold is indispensable at work, when a chap with a round of golf to play is not.

Women, on the other hand, really are indispensable. They have no choice but to be at the school gate, however ill they feel. So they are more likely to swallow a couple of painkillers and soldier on.

Hypochondriacs are not necessarily selfish. They can show touching, if overprotective concern for the health of friends and family. When my grandson Max had his birthday party at the local swimming pool, the father of one young guest was worried in case his daughter caught a cold staying in the water too long. 'You needn't worry,' said Max's mum, 'they keep the water terribly warm.' 'Oh dear,' the hypochondriac father replied, 'the ideal breeding ground for germs.'

To some women, and I'm afraid I'm one of them, the Florence Nightingale role doesn't come easily. We can't help thinking the patient is making a fuss about nothing. In my opinion, the best way to deal with a member of the family suffering from a *maladie imaginaire* is to make being ill as boring and uncomfortable as possible. Don't replace the hot-water bottle, don't shush the children, don't provide a radio or newspaper, do forget to buy Lucozade, and do vacuum the carpet in the bedroom when the patient is trying to doze. Above all, don't ask how they're feeling or give them a telephone so they can tell someone else.

If there is one hypochondriac in the extended family, there really should be a second one. Then, at family gatherings they can sit together (out of the draught, of course) and trade symptoms and remedies to their hearts' content. But if you only have one, and the burden seems too great, I can only suggest that you pre-empt it by saying, 'I've just been to see poor Mrs Grundy. You know she had to have her leg off.'

———————

At death's door

'No, Caudle; I wouldn't wish to say anything to accuse you; no, goodness knows, I wouldn't make you uncomfortable for the world — but the cold I've got, I got ten years ago... I was waiting for you; and I fell asleep, and the fire went out, and when I woke I found I was sitting right in the draught of the keyhole. That was my death, Caudle, though don't let that make you uneasy, love; for I don't think you meant to do it.

Ha! It's all very well for you to call it nonsense; and to lay your ill conduct upon my shoes. That's like a man, exactly! There never was a man yet that killed his wife, who couldn't give a good reason for it. No: I don't mean to say that you've killed me: quite the reverse: still, there's never been a day that I haven't felt that keyhole. What? Why won't I have a doctor? What's the use of a doctor? Why should I put you to expense? Besides, I dare say you'll do very well without me, Caudle: yes, after a very little time, you won't miss me much — no man ever does.

Peggy tells me, Miss Prettyman called today. What of it? Nothing, of course. Yes; I know she heard I was ill, and that's why she came. A little indecent, I think, Mr Caudle; She might wait; I

shan't be in her way long; she may soon have the
key of the caddy, now.

Mrs Caudle's Curtain Lectures,
Douglas Jerrold (1846)

For worse, she says

Once when he was feeling poorly, my husband checked
his temperature at frequent intervals, including at 3.45
am, waking the baby in the process. Of course it was
normal, and I was unsympathetic. He said, 'If only
my mum wasn't away, I'd go and stay with her. She'd
look after me.'

♥

My partner flatly refuses to blow his nose on a tissue; he
thinks tissues are for wimps — real men don't use them -
and insists on using handkerchiefs. Guess who has to wash
and iron them?

♥

He acts the noble and heroic type, going about his
normal business with heavy sighs and groans, glancing
covertly at me to see if I appreciate his plight. If I suggest
he goes to bed, he snaps at me, but if I ask him to do a
small chore, he closes his eyes with a resigned air, as if
to say, 'I have struggled bravely onward, but this… this…
will be the final straw that breaks my poor, quivering
back.'

♥

When he's got a cold he's even more of a misery than usual! I try and coax him back into a good mood with a cuddle and a hot toddy.

♥

He recently gave up smoking, and now has 'terrible chest pains'. He's convinced they're caused by lack of nicotine.

On the plus side, bad patients are often good nurses, and when it's our turn to be smitten with the flu bug, his loving concern and attempts to make us comfortable may put us to shame, and we may resolve to be more sympathetic next time he's ill.

February 11th, 1962   Sitting alone in the Gowings' 'oak room', church bells cascading outside; it's nearly six o'clock. I've enjoyed being here, though uneasily worrying whether I'm de trop – Lawrence being in bed, and Julia anxious about him. Following on the headlines 'TICKLE IN LAWRENCE'S THROAT', we now have 'LAWRENCE'S NOSE DEFINITELY RED AND SORE'. The fuss that arises from such slight malaise has clouded the air, as well as keeping Julia on the hop up and down stairs with trays and preoccupations.

**Julia – a Portrait of Julia Strachey,
by Herself and Frances Partridge (1983)**

Sickness isn't always purely physical, and when one partner is mentally or emotionally troubled, a sympathetic attitude on the part off the other may be very important. In Shakespeare's *Julius Caesar*, Brutus's loving wife Portia begs her husband to tell her what is wrong. She is trying to tell him that she married him for worse as well as for better, in sickness as well as in health, and she wants to share his burden:

> *No, my Brutus,*
> *You have some sick offence within your mind,*
> *Which by right and virtue of my place*
> *I ought to know of. And upon my knees,*
> *I charm [implore] you, by my once-commended beauty,*
> *By all your vows of love, and that great vow*
> *Which did incorporate and make us one,*
> *That you unfold to me, your self, your half,*
> *Why you are heavy.*

[Brutus is reluctant to confide in her, and Portia continues]

> *Am I yourself*
> *But as it were in sort of limitation?*
> *To keep with you at meals, comfort your bed,*
> *And talk to you sometimes? Dwell I but in the suburbs*
> *Of your good pleasure? If it be not more,*
> *Portia is Brutus' harlot, not his wife.*

In Health. . .

Even when in the best of health we should beware of giving the unspoken message, 'Accept me as I am, warts and all.'

When we live with someone very closely for years, it's easy to become lazy and not to make the sort of effort we would if we were single. It then follows naturally that we become resentful of each other's laziness: we feel it implies a lack of respect for each other. There is a fine line between being so comfortable with someone that we don't feel we have to put on a show, and being a lazy frump who can't be bothered to show true respect and love.

'He nags me about being a bit overweight – well, more than a bit, I suppose,' says a wife. 'He says he does love me the way I am – cuddly, but it's not good for my health. He gave me a subscription to the local gym for my birthday (so romantic – thanks a bundle!), and I do try to go once a week, but it's sometimes just too difficult to find the time, and then he thinks I'm making excuses, and we have a row about it.'

A husband complains: 'I'm pretty fit but I do smoke and drink, and she just can't accept it. I've told her again and again that I'm aware of the risks and there's no way I'm going to kick either habit. But she still just can't resist banging on about it. Hardly a week goes by without her pointing to some statistic in the paper about deaths from lung cancer, or telling me about someone in her office who had acupuncture to give up smoking. She's even worse about alcohol. She doesn't say anything, just silently holds the wine bottle up to the light and looks at the level.'

Good health, in the negative sense of absence of illness, is one of life's blessings, and we take it for granted at our peril. Positive, rude health, as advertised by the makers of vitamin pills and live yoghurt, is an extra bonus, and it's true, paradoxically, that the more fighting fit we are, the less likely we are to fight. If we're both bursting with energy, we're more likely to get out and about together and enjoy family life. So good health is good for marriage.

It is not so good, however, when health becomes an obsession. If one or both is constantly worrying about a diet, or spending too much time working out alone when they could be having fun together, it can have a negative effect on the relationship. Solve the problem by joining forces.

Go for a run or a swim together, and spend time in the kitchen jointly devising delicious ways of cooking the stipulated five-a-day fruit and veg.

...And in Absence

It may not be just ill health that keeps couples apart. Travel, for work or pleasure, can be a cause of tension too.

In the past, one of the great compensations of being apart, whether for a few days or for years at a time, was the love letter. Now we have emails, text messages, or a hasty conversation on a mobile phone that fades in and out of range – poor substitutes for the beloved's passion poured out over several handwritten pages. There are probably couples that don't even know what each other's writing looks like.

Every day every hour every moment makes me feel more deeply how blessed we are in each other, how purely how faithfully how ardently, and how tenderly we love each other; I put this last word last because, though I am persuaded that a deep affection is not uncommon in married life, yet I am confident that a lively, gushing, thought-employing, spirit-stirring passion of love, is very rare even among good people... We have been parted my sweet Mary too long, but we have not been parted in vain, for wherever I go I am admonished how blessed, and almost peculiar a lot mine is...

O Mary I love you with a passion of love which grows till I tremble to think of its strength; your children and the care which they require must fortunately steal between you and the solitude and the longings of absence – when I am moving about in travelling I am less unhappy than when stationary, but then I am at every moment, I will not say reminded of you, for you never I think are out of my mind 3 minutes together however I am engaged, but I am every moment seized with a longing wish that you might see the objects which interest me as I pass along, and not having you at my side my pleasure is so imperfect that after a short look I had rather not see the objects at all.

Letter from William Wordsworth to his wife Mary, soon after their fifth child was born, 11 August 1810

Yet I do not regret that this separation has been, for it is worth no small sacrifice to be thus assured, that instead of weakening, our union has strengthened — a hundred fold strengthened those yearnings towards each other which I used so strongly to feel at Gallows Hill — & in which you sympathized with me at that time — that these feelings are mutual now, I have the fullest proof, from thy letters & from their power & the power of absence over my whole frame — Oh William I can not tell thee how I love thee, & thou must not desire it — but feel it, O feel it in the fullness of thy soul & believe that I am the happiest of Wives & of Mothers & of all Women the most blessed... But I must stop or I know not whither I shall be carried & instead of composing myself by retiring I shall unfit myself for receiving the Party from Hereford

whom we are expecting —
Letter from Mary to William, two years later 23 May 1812

My generation used to listen for the sound of envelopes dropping from the letter-box on to the floor, experiencing a dull ache when the post turned out to contain nothing but bills, or a euphoric thrill at the sight of a foreign stamp and the dear, familiar writing.

A modern couple explains, 'Because of work, we're apart a lot, and although we stay in touch by phone and email for daily news, we write long letters to each other as well.' They find it a deeply satisfying way to focus on all that is good in their relationship and all that they love about each other, and are able to describe thoughts and emotions that they are too shy to speak of face to face.

My much loved Friend
I dare not express to you, at three hundred miles'
distance, how ardently I long for your return. I
have some very miserly wishes, and cannot consent
to your spending one hour in town, till, at least,
I have had you twelve. The idea plays about my
heart, unnerves my hand, whilst I write, — awakens
all the tender sentiments, that years have increased

and matured, and which, when with me, were every day dispensing to you. The whole collected stock of ten weeks' absence knows not how to brook any longer restraint, but will break forth and flow through my pen.

Letter to John Adams (second US president) from his wife Abigail, 16 October 1774

Next month completes three years that I have been devoted to the service of liberty. A slavery it has been to me, whatever the world may think of it. To a man whose attachments to his family are as strong as mine, absence alone from such a wife and such children would be a great sacrifice.... All other hard things I despise, but the loss of your company and that of my dear babes for so long a time, I consider as a loss of so much solid happiness. The tender social feelings of my heart, which have distressed me beyond all utterance in my most busy active scenes as well as in the numerous hours of melancholy solitude, are known only to God and my own soul.

Letter to Abigail from John Adams, June 1777

I reopen my envelope to tell you I have recd your dear letter of the 28th. I reciprocate intensely the feelings of love & devotion you show to me. My greatest good fortune in a life of brilliant experience has been to find you, & to lead my life with you. I don't feel far away from you out here at all. I feel vy near in my heart; & also I feel that the nearer I get to honour, the nearer I am to you.

Letter from Winston Churchill to his wife Clementine, 1915

I was glad to come home, & feel my real life coming back again — I mean life here with L. Solitary is not quite the right word; one's personality seems to echo out across space, when he's not there to enclose all one's vibrations. This is not very intelligibly written; but the feeling itself is a strange one — as if marriage were a completing of the instrument, & the sound of one alone penetrates as if it were a violin robbed of its orchestra or piano A dull wet night, so I shall sleep. The raid happened of course, with us away.

The Diary of Virginia Woolf, 2 November 1917 [She and Leonard had been married five years, and he was away for a few days, on a lecture tour]

The phone call from a restaurant on the other side
of the world reporting on the foie gras and lobster
thermidor, just when the hyperactive children have got
out of bed for the third time that night...

...can quickly dampen any fond feelings
for the absent one.

Does absence always make the heart grow fonder? Not necessarily. When complete trust between two people is lacking, it can put a strain on their relationship. If a partner's business trip takes them somewhere with a better climate, in convivial company, eating well and drinking well, all expenses paid, while the other is left literally holding the baby, it's understandable that the home-bound partner will feel they have drawn the short straw. Resentment breeds suspicion, and before long, doubts appear about that brunette in marketing whose neckline is always a little too low. The phone call from a restaurant on the other side of the world reporting on the foie gras and lobster thermidor, just when the hyper-active children have got out of bed for the third time that night, can quickly dampen any fond feelings for the absent one. We know such thoughts are unworthy of us, but we just can't help it. And then, when he arrives home jet-lagged, with a hangover, and demanding a lie-in on Saturday morning...

———◆◦◦◦◦◦◦◆———

One was married to some one. That one was going away to have a good time. The one that was married to that one did not like it very well that the one to whom that one was married then was going off alone to have a good time and was leaving that one to stay at home then. The one that was going came in all glowing. The one that was going had everything he was needing to have the good time he was wanting to be having then. He came in all glowing. The one he was leaving at home to take care of the family living was not glowing.

Portraits and Prayers, Gertrude Stein (1934)

———◦◦◦———

On the other hand, perhaps the prospect of a few days alone is a happy one. Time to get through a lot of chores. A chance to dine on toast and Marmite with bread and jam for pudding, then curl up with a bottle of wine in front of a silly TV programme or to go to bed early with a novel. Time to ring up an old schoolfriend and talk for an hour, or get the stepladder out and change the bulb in the hall light. It may be a good moment to consider a full-on beauty treatment – highlights, face-pack with cucumber slices on each eye, fingernails, toenails, the works.

The important thing – whether you are someone who is able to take proper advantage of the break or more of a moocher, ever conscious that someone is missing – is to enjoy the reunion. All of us will know the problem. When that someone finally comes home, even if we have felt the lack of them dreadfully, we are just not as pleased as we expected to be!

Give me to drink Mandragora...
That I may sleep out that great gap of time
My Antony is away.
Cleopatra in *Antony and Cleopatra*, William
Shakespeare

In fact there is a certain amount of bristling resentment that so much room is taken up, so much mess made so quickly; and surely there was a laundry service in the hotel that could have dealt with that suitcase full of dirty washing?

We mustn't judge too harshly. It might seem that the partner having a high old time with colleagues in one of the great cities of Europe showed a lack of consideration for the one left at home. But the absent one may see it differently: four days in non-stop meetings with dull workmates, hardly seeing daylight, let alone visiting the cathedral or shopping for presents for the children. The air-con has brought on hay fever and the jet-lag is terrible.

Make allowances for each other's minor difficulties. It may take a couple of days for things to get back to normal. Next time one or the other goes away, it just might be worth spending the lonely wee small hours writing each other love letters.

What is so torturing when I leave you at these London stations and drive off, is the knowledge that you are still there — that, for half an hour or three-quarters of an hour, I could still return and find you; come up behind you, take you by the elbow, and say 'Hadji'. [her affectionate name for him]

I came straight home, feeling horribly desolate and sad, driving down that familiar and dreary road. I remembered Rasht and our parting there: our parting at Victoria when you left for Persia; till our life seemed made up of partings, and I wondered how long it would continue.

Then I came round the corner on to the view — our view — and I thought how you loved it, and how simple you were, really, apart from your activity; and how I loved you for being both simple and active in one and the same person.

Then I came home, and it was no consolation at all. You see, when I am unhappy for other reasons, the cottage is a real solace to me; but when it is on account of you that I am unhappy (because you have gone away), it is an additional pang — it is the same place, but a sort of mockery and emptiness hangs about it — I almost wish that just once you could lose me and then come straight back to the cottage and find it still full of me but empty of me, then you would know what I go through after you have gone away.

Anyway, you will say, it is worse for you who go back to a horrible and alien city, whereas I stay in the place we both love so much; but really, Hadji, it is no consolation to come back to a place full of coffee-cups — there was a cardboard-box lid, full of your rose-petals, still on the terrace...

Darling, there are not many people who would write such a letter after sixteen years of marriage, yet who would be saying therein only one-fiftieth of what they were feeling as they wrote it. I sometimes try to tell you the truth, and then I find that I have no words at my command which could possible convey it to you.

Letter from Vita Sackville-West to Harold Nicolson, 25th June 1929

TO HIS WIFE ON THE 14TH
ANNIVERSARY OF HER WEDDING-DAY

'Thee, Mary, with this ring I wed,'
So, fourteen years ago, I said.
Behold another ring! 'For what?'
To wed thee o'er again – why not?

With that first ring I married youth,
Grace, beauty, innocence, and truth;
Taste long admired, sense long revered,
And all my Molly then appeared.

If she, by merit since disclosed,
Prove twice the woman I supposed,
I plead that double merit now,
To justify a double vow.

Here then, today (with faith as sure,
With ardour as intense and pure,
As when amidst the rites divine
I took thy troth, and plighted mine),
To thee, sweet girl, my second ring,
A token, and a pledge, I bring;
With this I wed, till death us part,
Thy riper virtues to my heart;
Those virtues which, before untried,
The wife has added to the bride…

Samuel Bishop (1731-95)

8
TILL DEATH US DO PART

When two people are under the influence of the most violent, most insane, most delusive, and most transient of passions, they are required to swear that they will remain in that excited, abnormal and exhausting condition continuously until death do them part.

Getting Married, George Bernard Shaw (1908)

In days gone by marriages were shorter than they are today, not because of divorce but because people died younger. So 'until death us do part' may not have been a very long time at all. If widows and widowers did remarry, they tended to do so in spite of the fact that choice was limited – many people did not venture beyond their own village or town when looking for a husband or wife.

Times have changed. Internet dating and ease of travel mean that anyone looking for a partner is spoilt for choice. This fact alone makes it harder to stay happily married to the same person. The grass can seem such a brilliant shade of green outside the marriage. 'Marriage is a wonderful institution,' as Groucho Marx put it, 'but who wants to live in an institution?' The writer Arnold Bennett felt something of the same and believed that the horror of marriage lay in its 'dailiness'. He wrote that 'the too close and too constant companionship of the twain, who simply get sick of one another' caused the erosion of most marriages. It certainly seems to have applied to his own, which only lasted 14 years before he left his wife for another woman.

Nevertheless, these days it's not unusual for a couple to notch up 40 years together (a ruby anniversary), or even 50 (golden). Rob and I have only three years to go to reach our half century. How have we managed to stay the course?

Ringing the Changes

Marriage is the alliance of two people, one of whom never remembers birthdays and the other never forgets them.
Ogden Nash

WEDDING ANNIVERSARIES

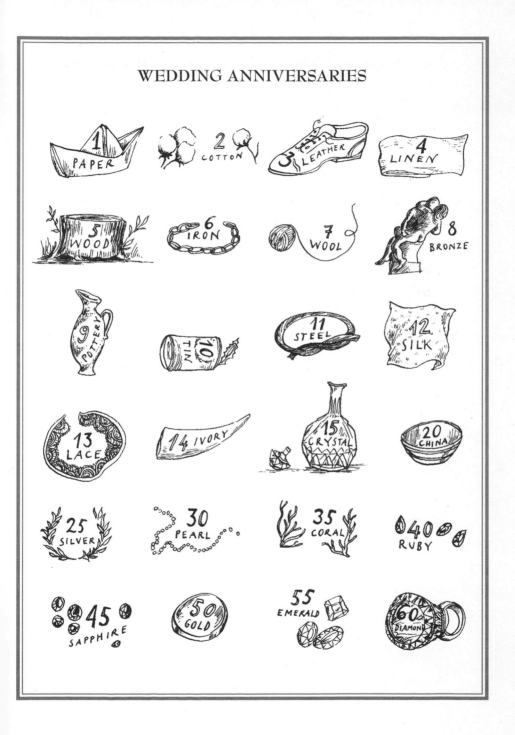

The answer to an enduring marriage, according to Virginia Woolf, was not to fear the monotony of spending years with the same person, but to embrace it, to see it as a source of potential and strength: 'The truth is more like this: Life – say four days out of seven – becomes automatic; but on the fifth day a bead of sensation (between husband and wife) forms which is all the fuller and more sensitive because of the automatic customary unconscious days on either side. That is to say the year is marked by moments of great intensity.'

If the moments of intensity come too few and far between, one or both partners may wonder if there is any point in staying married for the rest of their lives. A wife admits: 'After six years I was bored, bored, bored with spending all day with two pre-school children. I didn't want to broach the subject with my partner because I was scared of letting the genie out of the bottle, but we finally talked it through and, as we have no family nearby to help with the children, we agreed to get a regular babysitter so we could go out and have time together. Things are better between us already, and I'm hoping they'll continue to improve.'

It's the sameness of daily life that causes people to attach great importance to landmarks in their lives. Why else should some people consider it a crime to forget the card, the red roses and the evening out on a wedding anniversary, on Valentine's Day, on birthdays or other supposedly memorable occasions? Each year of marriage is certainly an achievement worth celebrating, and marking the anniversary is a good way to alleviate the 'dailiness' of married life. For certain men, it used to be thanks to the secretary that these big events were remembered at all. Perhaps it still is, in some circles. But likely as not, if important dates mean a great deal to either one of the couple, heavy hints have to be dropped or, less romantically, events have to be organised by the more practical of the two.

The routine of the early years of our own marriage, in the 1960s, was rather pleasurable. For stay-at-home mothers (and there were more of us in those days), the day was made up of shopping, cooking, washing, ironing, nappy changing and feeding children. Although I never found these activities particularly fulfilling, I relished the perks of being at home. I blush to think of it now, but I spent happy afternoons watching soaps on TV while the children napped. *Peyton Place*, starring Mia Farrow, was my favourite, with some knitting or sewing on my lap to salve my conscience.

Today most mothers work and their routine is very different. And yet juggling a job with home and children, hectic and stress-laden as it is, can be just as monotonous as a more leisurely life. The daily grind can still be soul-destroying. And marriage-destroying. A disillusioned wife writes: 'We've been together for nearly eight years, and familiarity is starting to breed contempt. I know it's my fault, not his. He's done nothing wrong but he just irritates me for no apparent reason. If I'm not careful I snap his head off and I have to bite my tongue when I hear the same old jokes and saying... I feel like a bitch and I'm hoping this will pass and we'll get back to normal.'

There's a good chance it will pass, although couples seldom become less irritated by each other as the years go by. On the contrary, according to recent research among couples of all age groups, the longer people are together the more annoying they find their partner. The good news is that partners can learn to live with the irritation, and, via tolerance, end up feeling closer and more comfortable with each other.

It's worth remembering that a partner him or herself is not necessarily the source of the irritation. The true reason may be that the bathwater was cold, the mother-in-law rang at the wrong moment, or the children were whingeing all day.

Marriage is one long conversation, chequered by disputes...The whole material of life is turned over and over, ideas are struck out and shared, the two persons more and more adapt their notions one to suit the other, and in process of time, without sound of trumpet, they conduct each other into new worlds of thought.
Robert Louis Stevenson (1850-94)

In a long-lasting marriage, husband and wife can

expect to fall out of love at some point. This need not cause despair. It's normal and more often than not it's only temporary. It can happen more than once, and is absolutely not a sign that the marriage is over. Nearly all relationships go through bad patches from time to time but if both people show patience and understanding, it should lead to greater tolerance and deepened affection.

During the bad patches, consideration for each other is an invaluable tool. C. Northcote Parkinson wrote in *Mrs Parkinson's Law* (1968), 'Living together depends, above all, on courtesy.

The affection we have for other people should often make us more than courteous but it should never, surely, make us less. Kindness goes beyond politeness; it should not fall short of it. And this is the more important if we have children, for their ideas of politeness will derive mainly from example. The courtesy which they offer to others will be a reflection of what they experience at home. There is no greater mistake than to suppose that marriage frees us from the need to be polite. It rather does the opposite, demanding from us more than politeness in circumstances when our temptation is to offer less.'

If we are unfailingly polite to one another (except, of course, when having a blazing row), it will certainly do the relationship no harm, and it may do it good. If politeness and tolerance become ingrained, they are a self-perpetuating prophecy – act the part, and the feelings follow.

*After all, life was not made up of moments of
exaltation, but of quite ordinary, everyday things.
The visions of the shining, inaccessible peaks
vanished; Jenny remembered two pieces of domestic news, and told Adam about them. They were
not very romantic, but they were really much
more important than grand passions or blighted
loves: Giles Jonathan had cut his first tooth, and
Adam's best cow had given birth to a fine heifer-
calf.*

A Civil Contract, Georgette Heyer (1961)

In their early years together, couples want to spend as
much time as possible in each other's company, and either
one may resent the other's separate interests and pursuits.
If the one left at home is bored and resentful, there are two
things that can be done. Each can try and share the other's interests, however alien they may seem. Windsurfing
or line dancing just might become lifelong pleasures! Of
course, this plan won't always work. With the best will in
the world, a wife can't join the football team her husband
plays with every Saturday, and wild horses are unlikely to
drag him to her book club. In such cases, there is another
course of action. It couldn't be simpler: leave him to the
football and her to the book club. When they get home she
will agree that the ref was blind, and he will applaud her
penetrating analysis of Anna Karenina.

For better, they say

He's the only person I can stand spending a lot of time with, everyone else in the world gets on my nerves after a while… The fact that he can put up with and live with me the way I am and still love me just makes me feel we suit each other.

♥

We've been married 13 years, and I can honestly say our relationship is better than it's ever been. We've been through some really difficult times, and come out the other side. The key really is communication and not holding grudges.

♥

After 22 years together, if anything I love him more as we've shared more time together, both happy and sad. I'm a firm believer in working hard at a marriage. There will always be tough times when you can't abide each other but they make the good times better. Soppy, I know, but true.

♥

Over the years I've come to accept that boredom is part of marriage, just the same as in other aspects of life, but the highlights make it so worthwhile.

♥

I value above all the pleasurable companionship that comes from knowing each other inside out.

As the years go by, being together every moment may become less important and is not necessarily desirable. Far from wanting to live in each other's pockets, some couples long for an occasional rest from each other. It's perfectly natural to reach a stage when we are no longer so keen to sit in on the poker game, walk round the golf course, or listen to our beloved spouting Latin plant names in National Trust gardens. A time will come when we are only too glad to be excused so we can do our own thing.

May 4th [1948]
I quite often look back at the pleasures and pains of youth — love, jealousy, recklessness, vanity — without forgetting their spell but no longer desiring them; while middle-aged ones like music, places, botany, conversation seem to be just as enjoyable as those wilder ones, in which there was usually some potential anguish lying in wait, like a bee in a flower. I hope there may be further surprises in store, and on the whole do not fear the advance into age ...
Everything to lose: Diaries 1945-60,
Frances Partridge

'Honey, I'm Home – For ever!'

The old couple were as absorbed in themselves as lovers, content and self-contained; they never left the village or each other's company, they lived as snug as two podded chestnuts. By day blue smoke curled up from their chimney, at night the red windows glowed; the cottage, when we passed it, said 'Here live the Browns', as though that were part of nature...

When they moved about in their tiny kitchen they did so smoothly and blind, gliding on worn, familiar rails, never bumping or obstructing each other. They were fond, pink-faced, and alike as cherries, having taken and merged, through their years together, each other's looks and accents.

Cider with Rosie, Laurie Lee (1959)

How lucky were the Browns. For many couples, retirement greatly increases the potential for friction. When both partners are working, they only live in close proximity in the evenings and at weekends, and their working lives provide them with plenty to talk about. After retirement, unless they make other arrangements, they are together day in day out, seven days a week.

It's a notoriously difficult time, especially for people whose working life has been interesting, challenging and demanding. Most couples look forward to the time when they will have leisure to do all the things they never got around to. But instead of spending golden days together, it can turn out that, if one partner is happy and occupied, the other is at a loose end. I remember my grandmother being cheerfully busy around the house while my grandfather gazed mournfully out of the window, jingling the loose change in his pocket. 'He gets under my feet,' she would complain 'I can't be doing with it', as she manoeuvred the vacuum cleaner around his feet.

Freed, after 45 years or so, from working life, some people are unable to decide just what it is they really would like to do with all the time at their disposal. Sudoku and *Countdown* may keep the grey matter ticking over, but they hardly rate as fulfilment for someone accustomed to the battles of the boardroom. An occasional round of golf with fellow oldies is not much better…

It need not be like that. Research undertaken by Australian psychologist Michael Longhurst has shown that people who engage in five hours or more a week of 'purposeful' activity were less likely to suffer retirement-related anxiety, stress or depression, and that their experience of retirement was far more rewarding.

For anyone missing the buzz of a work environment, it is possible to return part-time to that world, perhaps in a voluntary job. Or take up a sport that there was never time for while working. Or learn tap-dancing or yoga. One couple of my acquaintance spend their annual holiday on a cruise where they can indulge their two passions: bridge and ballroom dancing. Of course you don't have to be on a cruise ship to play cards or dance. But whatever the new activity, it's important to start it no more than a year from the date of retirement, before inertia sets in.

*Whatever the new activity, it's important to start it
no more than a year from the date of retirement,
before inertia sets in.*

For anyone who retires without knowing how to operate a computer, I'd make lessons compulsory. The internet opens so many doors, from investigating family history to checking out batting records in Test cricket, to making a garden pond, or simply keeping in touch with far-flung friends and family by email.

Activities and new pursuits, however fun and diverting, though, cannot answer all one's needs. In retirement, you should also simply be able to fall back on years of companionship. Frank Longford – interviewed in *The English Marriage* by Drusilla Beyfus – pointed out that, towards the end of a long and happy marriage, the two people involved will have so much in common, so many memories, so many interests, so many friends that they really should have plenty to talk about in a serious way, quite apart from the private jokes that will have accumulated.

'There is no substitute for the comfort supplied by the utterly taken-for-granted relationship,' Iris Murdoch wrote in *A Severed Head* (1976). Happily married couples develop a rapport that amounts to telepathy so that, in company, they can communicate by catching each other's eye in a way that's invisible to everyone else, and when alone, they know what the other is about to say before they speak.

As Time Goes by… Some Testimonials

Surveys show that people who are married live longer. They are also people, it ought to be said, who tend to eat breakfast, wear seat belts, take exercise, have their blood pressure checked and are less likely to smoke than widows and widowers. But the time must eventually come when death will tear them apart. And as that eventuality draws closer, writers have felt the need to express their feelings about marriage, committing their words to diaries, in letters to their beloved, in prose and in verse. Here is a selection, to show what a long and happy marriage can mean.

To darling Carlotta, my wife, who for twenty-three years has endured with love and understanding my rotten nerves, my lack of stability, my cussed-ness in general...

I am old and would be sick of life, were it not that you, Sweetheart, are here, as deep and under-standing in your love as ever — and I as deep in my love for you as when we stood in Paris, Premier Arrondissement on July 22, 1929, and both said faintly 'Oui'!

Dedication on the flyleaf of *Moon for the Misbegotten* by Eugene O'Neill, July 1952

My own dear Husband, If I should depart this life before you, leave orders that we may be buried in the same grave at whatever distance you may die

from England. And now, God bless you, my kindest, dearest! You have been a perfect husband to me. Be put by my side in the same grave. And now, fare- well, my dear Dizzy. Do not live alone, dearest. I earnestly hope you may find someone as attached to you as your own devoted Mary Anne.

Letter from Lady Beaconsfield to her husband, Benjamin Disraeli, Earl of Beaconsfield (1856)

*To whom I owe the leaping delight
That quickens my senses in our wakingtime
And the rhythm that governs the repose of our sleepingtime,
The breathing in unison.*

*Of lovers whose bodies smell of each other
Who think the same thoughts without need of speech,
And babble the same speech without need of meaning.*

*No peevish winter wind shall chill
No sullen tropic sun shall wither
The roses in the rose-garden which is ours and ours only
But this dedication is for others to read:
These are private words addressed to you in public.*

A Dedication to my Wife, T.S. Eliot (1958)

At the sea-end of town, Mr and Mrs Floyd, the cocklers, are sleeping as quiet as death, side by wrinkled side, toothless, salt and brown, like two old kippers in a box.

Under Milk Wood, Dylan Thomas (1954)

When you are old and grey and full of sleep,
And nodding by the fire, take down this book,
And slowly read, and dream of the soft look
Your eyes had once, and of their shadows deep;

How many loved your moments of glad grace,
And loved your beauty with love false or true,
But one man loved the pilgrim soul in you,
And loved the sorrows of your changing face;

And bending down beside the glowing bars,
Murmur, a little sadly, how Love fled
And paced upon the mountains overhead
And hid his face amid a crowd of stars.

'When You Are Old', W.B. Yeats (1906)

He first deceased; she for a little tried
To live without him, liked it not, and died.

Upon the Death of Sir Albertus Morton's Wife, Sir Henry Wotton (1568-1639)

We've been together now for forty years
And it don't seem a day too much.
There ain't a lady livin' in the land
As I'd swop for my dear old Dutch.
Words by A.C. Ingle Music, Albert
Chevalier (1911)

After the Golden Wedding
(Three Soliloquies)

1. The husband's

She's not a faultless woman; no!
She's not an angel in disguise:
She has her rivals here below:
She's not an unexampled prize:

She does not always see the point
Of little jests her husband makes:
And, when the world is out of joint,
She makes a hundred small mistakes:

She's not a miracle of tact:
Her temper's not the best I know:
She's got her little faults in fact,
Although I never tell her so.

But this, my wife, is why I hold you
As good a wife as ever stepped,

And why I meant it when I told you
How cordially our feast I kept:

You've lived with me these fifty years,
And all the time you loved me dearly:
I may have given you cause for tears:
I may have acted rather queerly.

I ceased to love you long ago:
Loved another for a season:
As time went on I came to know
Your worth, my wife: and saw the reason

Why such a wife as you have been
Is more than worth the world beside;
You loved me all the time, my Queen;
You couldn't help it if you tried.

You loved me as I once loved you,
As each loved each beside the altar:
And whatsoever I might do,
Your loyal heart could never falter.

And, if you sometimes fail me, sweetest,
And don't appreciate me, dear,
No matter: such defects are meetest
For poor humanity, I fear.

And all's forgiven, all's forgot,
On this our golden wedding day;
For, see! she loves me: does she not?
So let the world e'en go its way.

I'm old and nearly useless now,

Each day a greater weakling proves me:
There's compensation anyhow:
I still possess a wife that loves me.

2. The wife's

Dear worthy husband! good old man!
Fit hero of a golden marriage:
I'll show towards you, if I can,
An absolutely wifely carriage.

The months or years which your career
May still comprise before you perish,
Shall serve to prove that I, my dear,
Can honour, and obey, and cherish.

Till death us part, as soon he must,
(And you, my dear, should shew the way)
I hope you'll always find me just
The same as on our wedding day.

I never loved you, dearest, never!
Let that be clearly understood:
I thought you good, and rather clever,
And found you really rather good.

And what was more, I loved another,
But couldn't get him: well, but, then
You're just as bad, my erring brother,
You most impeccable of men: —

Except for this: my love was married

Some weeks before I married you:
While you, my amorous dawdler, tarried
Till we'd been wed a year or two.

You loved me at our wedding: I
Loved someone else: and after that
I never cast a loving eye
On others: you — well, tit for tat!

But after all I made you cheerful:
Your whims I've humoured: saw the point
Of all your jokes: grew duly tearful,
When you were sad, yet chose the joint

You liked the best of all for dinner,
And soothed you in your hours of woe:
Although a miserable sinner,
I am a good wife, as wives go.

I bore with you and took your side,
And kept my temper all the time:
I never flirted; never cried,
Nor ranked it as a heinous crime,

When you preferred another lady,
Or used improper words to me,
Or told a story more than shady,
Or snored and snorted after tea,

Or otherwise gave proofs of being
A dull and rather vain old man:

I still succeeded in agreeing
With all you said (the safest plan).

Had love been wanted — well, I couldn't
Have given what I'd not to give;
Or had a genius asked me! wouldn't
The man have suffered? now, we live

Among our estimable neighbours
A decent and decorous life:
I've earned by my protracted labours
The title of a model wife.

But when beneath the turf you're sleeping,
And I am sitting here in black
Engaged, as they'll suppose, in weeping,
I shall not wish to have you back.

3. The vicar's
A good old couple! kind and wise!
And oh! what love for one another!
They've won, those two, life's highest prize,
Oh! let us copy them, my brother.

James Kenneth Stephen (1891)

Dearest, it worries me vy much that you
should seem to nurse such absolutely wild suspicions
wh are so dishonouring to all the love & loyalty I bear
you & will please god bear you while I breathe. They are
unworthy of you & me. And they fill my mind with feelings
of embarrassment to wh I have been a stranger since I was a
schoolboy. I know that they originate in the fond love you have
for me, and therefore they make me feel tenderly towards you &
anxious always to deserve that most precious possession of my life.
But at the same time they depress me & vex me – & without reason.

We do not live in a world of small intrigues, but of serious &
important affairs. I could not conceive myself forming any other
attachment than that to which I have fastened the happiness of my life
here below. And it offends my best nature that you should – against
your true instinct – indulge small emotions & wounding doubts. You
ought to trust me for I do not love & will never love any woman in the
world but you and my chief desire is to link myself to you week by
week by bonds which shall ever become more intimate & profound.

Beloved I kiss your memory – your sweetness & beauty
have cast a glory upon my life.
You will find me always your loving & devoted husband
W

**Winston S. Churchill, letter to his wife
(November 1909)**

9
FORSAKING ALL OTHERS

Hogamous, higamous
Man is polygamous
Higamus, hogamous
Woman monogamous
William James (1842-1910)

High Fidelity

Should couples, in the words of the Christian marriage service, forsake all others and keep only to their spouse? Put more simply, should they remain faithful to each other? With very few exceptions, everyone I have asked, both men and women, felt strongly that they should. Here are some of their reasons:

> *Sex and physical intimacy are a massive part of a good relationship; they brought us together in the first place and*

are precious because they are just for us, and not shared with anyone else.

♥

When we made our vows we promised to be faithful. If we're going to break our vows, what's the point of getting married in the first place?

♥

Trust is all-important, once trust breaks down it's a slippery slope. I would never see my partner in the same light afterwards, especially if it was better with someone else.

♥

Extra-marital affairs can never work and should be avoided at all costs — they can only bring great unhappiness for everyone, including the children.

♥

If you want to shag around you shouldn't be in a serious relationship. You've made a choice to be with your partner, so fantasise if you must, but don't make the fantasy real.

♥

An affair, even one the spouse doesn't know about, is completely toxic to a marriage. If you are unfaithful in secret, you will be living a lie for the rest of your married life.

♥

Three people in a relationship doesn't work — it's just not fair to bring a 'sexual competitor' into the marital equation.

♥

*If you constantly have your eye on others, it puts your
commitment to your partner in question. But during decades of marriage an affair or two shouldn't be considered
grounds for divorce.*

♥

*Our ten years together have whizzed by — we laugh
together all the time and I still fancy him hugely. He is
everything to me and although we do argue I can't
imagine life without him. The fact that we have both
been faithful during our relationship is something we
both agree makes things more special.*

So if most people, men as well as women, agree that
faithfulness is highly desirable, do they practise what
they preach? Who knows? One of the few dissenters from
the general point of view insisted that the real command-
ment is 'Thou shalt not be found out.' Another, ready
to own up to occasional indiscretions on business trips
abroad, felt that lapses in which there is no emotional
involvement should be excused. The actor Bette Davis
was more outspoken: 'An affair now and then is good
for a marriage. It adds spice, stops it from getting boring
… I ought to know.' Perhaps it shouldn't be so, but the
words people use when referring to sex often indicate a
difference in the way they perceive it; a man may put a
'quick shag' with someone in the office in a different category from 'making love' to his wife. But he would still
rather his wife didn't find out.

A few felt that an 'open' marriage could be a happy one, provided the rules of the relationship were agreed upon beforehand, and adhered to by both partners. The problem with that arrangement is that one partner usually ends up having more fun than the other.

An 18th-century view:

Johnson *Between a man and his wife, a husband's infidelity is nothing. They are connected by children, by fortune, by serious considerations of community. Wise married women don't trouble themselves about the infidelity of their husbands.*

Boswell *To be sure there is a great difference between the offence of infidelity in a man and that of his wife.*

Johnson *The difference is boundless. The man imposes no bastards upon his wife.*

Life of Samuel Johnson, **James Boswell (1791)**

In an ideal world, another couple agreed, partners should remain faithful, but they felt it was asking a lot to expect it throughout a long-lasting marriage. They considered occasional 'wandering' understandable although not desirable, but if it happened too often, the trust built up between them would be increasingly under threat. The consensus seems to be that, to put it crudely, a one-night stand can be treated as a regrettable hiccup, whereas a full-blown affair can seriously damage a marriage and may even end it.

The Seven-Year Itch

Do not adultery commit;
Advantage rarely comes of it.
Arthur Hugh Clough (1819-1861)

Given that it's considered such a big threat to a partnership, why is even the most devoted spouse sometimes tempted to stray from the straight and narrow path?

I think the most dangerous years really are the first ten years. Your husband hasn't become a habit in the sense of being an essential part of your life. He hasn't had time to... You could perfectly well have various affairs at the same time thinking your marriage is your basic one, and then to your surprise you may find one of the affairs outside has suddenly eclipsed your marriage, after you've been married about six or seven years. ...I do not see how [the marriage]

can develop unless you have long periods together when you really are isolated. By that I mean two or three evenings a week not going out. If I hear that young married couples go out every evening, even if they go out together, even if they start out together and come home together, I always think this is going to be dangerous.

Elizabeth Longford, quoted in *The English Marriage***, Drusilla Beyfus (1971)**

The average age of marriage for men is now nearly 33, and for women 30; the average age of divorce is nearly 42 for men, 39 for women. So it seems that, before finally splitting up, many couples spend a couple of years scratching the notorious seven-year-itch. (Billy Wilder's 1955 movie of that name is remembered for the iconic image of Marilyn Monroe standing over a subway ventilation grating, with her skirt blowing up around her.)

The seventh year of marriage is still a recognised danger zone, as wives and partners have explained:

Seven years into our relationship, we're starting to tell each other, "this conversation is boring and repetitive". We are starting to wonder, is this really the rest of our lives?'

♥

I had a little fling when we had been together seven years. I felt I was beginning to disappear into the wallpaper of

[238]

*my life and craved the excitement and danger of an affair,
but it didn't help in the slightest.*

♥

*Our relationship has never been very passionate, and
sometimes I wonder if we've both missed our chance for a
big romance or does that just happen in the movies?*

Seven years is a convenient peg on which to hang
the marital discontent that can occur even in the happiest marriages. It can happen at any time, and it can happen more than once. A wife explains, 'If you make it
past the seven-year itch, be prepared for it to hit again at
14 years. Now I've got over that, I'm wondering if the
next crisis will come after 21 years!' Another wife who
has notched up 18 years of happy marriage says there
have been times when she wanted to run away and live
on her own, and fall in love again with someone exciting and rich. 'But it's just a phase and it soon passes.
Anyway, where would I find the exciting, rich, new
man? I'm sure my husband has similar urges, too. You
just have to realise they're not important – the rest
of the time we get on really well, we enjoy each other's
company and make each other laugh a lot.'

> *Women, as well as men, ought to have a great many
> love affairs before they marry as the most critical
> moment in a marriage is the falling off of physical
> love, which is bound to occur sooner or later and
> only an experienced woman can know how to cope*

with this. If not properly dealt with the marriage is bound to go on the rocks.

Nancy Mitford: note in her appointments diary for 1941

Whether it comes after seven years or, as with one couple I know, 37 years, in most marriages there will be a time, perhaps more than one time, when the relationship comes under threat because one partner is discontented or simply bored. There is a wide variety of reasons why it happens. Some people resent the fact that, as they see it, their spouses take them for granted; others, ground down by the monotony of family life, long for the kind of adventure and romance they find in fiction.

Adultery can also be infectious. If a friend is having a deliriously happy, roller-coaster extra-marital affair, it is hard not to feel a little envious, and to yearn for a bit of the same.

He thought she was happy; and she hated him for that placid immobility, that stolid serenity of his, for that very happiness which she herself brought him...

She had no difficulty in persuading herself that there was nothing very startling now about

Charles' passion for her. His ardours had lapsed into a routine, his embraces kept fixed hours; it was just one more habit, a sort of dessert he looked forward to after the monotony of dinner. If matters had fallen out differently, she wondered, might she not have met some other man?

Madame Bovary, **Gustave Flaubert (1857)**

Oh, how deceptively lush the grass beyond the fence looks to the Madame Bovarys of this world! But for some women it's their own dullness rather than that of their husband that makes them hanker for a new love. Years of domesticity, childbearing and childcare have made them feel unsexy and dreary. If a new man shows that he's attracted to such a woman, she may find it hard to resist grasping the excitement an affair can offer, bringing reassurance that she is still desirable. However, she may not need a full-on affair to restore her self-esteem. Just to live dangerously may give her the thrill she craves. 'They mistake the matter much that think all adultery is below the girdle,' John Donne wrote in his Sermons, 'a man darts out an adultery with his eye, in a wanton look; and he wraps up adultery with his fingers, in a wanton letter; and he breathes in an adultery with his lips, in a wanton kisse.'

A flirtation can be, in Donne's terms, just as sinful, and in our terms just as dangerous as a full sexual relationship. The most likely candidate for a 'harmless' flirtation is a former girlfriend or boyfriend. An old flame can seem very attractive to someone weighed down with domestic life. Where's the harm in meeting up for lunch, a gossip and an affectionate kiss for old times' sake? Probably no harm at all, but it's dangerous ground to tread. What if there is another meeting the following week, and the next, and the next? If an old flame appears, it isn't worth putting the family's happiness at risk by making a clandestine assignation. Don't be tempted. Instead, insist on asking the ex home to meet your spouse and children, thereby converting a dangerous old flame into a shared family friend.

LOOKING UP AN OLD FLAME? THINK TWICE

It sounds innocent. You get to wondering whatever happened to that special someone you dated in high school or college, so you track her, or him, down online and send an e-mail. Your old flame is thrilled to hear from you. You chat online, talk on the phone, meet for coffee. And faster than you ever imagined, everything gets out of hand and someone's marriage is ruined.

It happens a lot more often than you'd think.

'It starts with e-mails,' says Nancy Kalish, a psychology professor at Cal State Sacramento. 'It goes to IMs (instant messages), and the hotel room follows pretty soon afterward.'

C'mon, we're not talking about people looking for an affair, just a cup of coffee with an old friend. That may be the plan, but Kalish says that's not how it often works out. She's been charting hookups between lost loves since 1993, and says the internet has changed how such stories unfold.

Back in the 1990s, it was rare for a married person to reach out to a first love. Nowadays, about 8 in 10 people who contact a former lover are married. Of course, most of them don't intend to get into trouble when they log on, and not all of them do.

It's never been easier to look up and hook up with an old crush. But if you're in a relationship, Kalish has three words for you.

Don't do it.

Old flames meet, they reconnect instantly and powerfully, and before long the situation has run away from them.

San Francisco Chronicle, 10 January, 2006

The Green-Eyed Monster

> *O! beware, my lord, of jealousy;*
> *It is the green-eyed monster which doth mock*
> *The meat it feeds on.*
>
> **Iago in *Othello*, William Shakespeare**
> **(1603)**

The destructive effect of unfaithfulness, whether real or, as in the case of Othello and Desdemona, imagined, is inflamed by the insidious emotion of jealousy. Jealous people not only begin to hate their partners for, as they suspect, two-timing them, they also begin to despise themselves, the more so when they find that, although they repeatedly tell themselves to snap out of being suspicious and possessive, they cannot.

> *Trifles light as air*
> *Are to the jealous confirmations strong*
> *As proofs of holy writ.*
>
> **Iago in *Othello*, William Shakespeare**
> **(1603)**

A husband, whose otherwise happy marriage has been marred by his wife's constant suspicion, says: 'During our seven years together we've been very happy but she's always been intensely jealous and distrustful of me. She can't bear to see me even talking to another woman, and frequently accuses me of having affairs, although I've given her no reason for suspicion and constantly reassure her of my love and fidelity.'

Anyone married to a natural flirt is doomed to a life of suspicion and jealousy unless they can accept that flirting is a character trait, not to be taken seriously. The partner who flirts is just keeping his hand in, as one might with any skill one is proud of, and anyone who makes a mountain out of such a molehill may end up feeling very foolish. If the flirting is taken seriously by one partner, there is a danger that the other will take his cue from that, and persuade himself that there is a more serious emotion underlying his automatic reaction to a pretty and lively companion.

Mrs Mantalini is jealous

'If you will be odiously, demnebly outrageously jealous, my soul,' said Mr Mantalini, 'you will be very miserable — horrid miserable — demnition miserable.' And then, there was a sound as though Mr Mantalini were sipping his coffee.

'I am miserable,' returned Madame Mantalini, evidently pouting.

'Then you are an ungrateful, unworthy, demd

unthankful little fairy,' said Mr Mantalini.

'I am not,' returned Madame, with a sob.

'Do not put itself out of humour,' said Mr Mantalini, breaking an egg. 'It is a pretty, bewitching little demd countenance, and it should not be out of humour, for it spoils its loveliness, and makes it cross and gloomy like a frightful, naughty, demd hobgoblin.'

'I am not to be brought round in that way, always,' rejoined Madame, sulkily.

'It shall be brought round in any way it likes best, and not brought round at all if it likes that better,' retorted Mr Mantalini, with his egg-spoon in his mouth.

'It's very easy to talk,' said Mrs Mantalini.

'Not so easy when one is eating a demnition egg,' replied Mr Mantalini; 'for the yolk runs down the waistcoat, and yolk of egg does not match any waistcoat but a yellow waistcoat, demit.'

'You were flirting with her during the whole night,' said Madame Mantalini, apparently desirous to lead the conversation back to the point from which it had strayed.

'No, no my life.'

'You were,' said Madame, 'I had my eye upon you all the time.

'Bless the little winking twinkling eye; was it on me all the time!' cried Mantalini, in a sort of lazy rapture. 'Oh, demmit!'

'And I say once more,' resumed Madame, 'that you ought not to waltz with anybody but your *own wife; and I will not bear it, Mantalini, if I take poison first.'*

'She will not take poison and have horrid pains, will she?' said Mantalini; who, by the altered sound of his voice, seemed to have moved his chair, and taken up his position nearer to his wife. 'She will not take poison, because she had a demd fine husband who might have married two countesses and a dowager —'

'Two countesses,' interposed Madame. 'You told me one before!'

'Two!' cried Mantalini. 'Two demd fine women, real countesses and splendid fortunes, demit.'

'And why didn't you?' asked Madame playfully.

'Why didn't I!' replied her husband. 'Had I not seen, at a morning concert, the demdest little fascinator in all the world, and while that little fascinator is my wife, may not all the countesses and dowagers in England be —' Mr Mantalini did not finish the sentence, but he gave Madame Mantalini a very loud kiss, which Madame Mantalini returned; after which, there seemed to be some more kissing mixed up with the progress of the breakfast.

Nicholas Nickleby, Charles Dickens (1839)

There is a form of jealousy, increasingly common in these days of relatively frequent divorce and remarriage, which focuses on the other's ex-husband or ex-wife. It's admirable, and, in fact, essential for their children's welfare, for divorced or separated couples to maintain a civilised and friendly relationship, but in this they cannot always count on the support, or even the neutrality of their new partners. The sound of merry laughter, when a husband or wife is on the telephone to the ex, can give the newcomer a jolt of jealous resentment which, if unchecked, can develop into constant, unwarranted criticism of the ex. 'Just look at the state of the children's clothes – you'd think she'd find time to iron them.' Or 'For heaven's sake, he knows I don't allow them to go swimming when they've got colds.' This kind of comment is not helpful. It's also never, ever right to slag off an ex to the children, or in front of them.

Reason says it's crazy to be jealous of a partner's ex. It's you he or she loves now, and if their relationship has converted successfully from past love to present friendship, it's a cause for rejoicing, not resentment. The trouble is, jealousy is not reasonable. It's usually based, like Othello's, on suspicion, not fact, and the best weapon against suspicion is the truth. Communication is always important and the best way to find something out is by asking. It's the unasked questions that cause trouble. The longer they remain unasked and unanswered, the worse the imagined scenario becomes. The person always wondering who is texting their spouse should ask. The answer may be unwelcome, but likely as not it will clear up a misunderstanding. Either way the subject is better brought into the open.

My wife's jealousy is getting ridiculous. The other day she looked at my calendar and wanted to know who May was.

Rodney Dangerfield (1921-2004)

Just occasionally, an affair is the symptom of an incurable fault in a marriage, and divorce may be the best possible outcome for all concerned. But in most cases, exposing the truth about an affair leads to its end – the secrecy and fear of being found out were part of the thrill, and once the truth is out, there is not much point in carrying on with it – and then the long road to reparation can begin.

It is also not necessarily right to come clean about an affair, however, even after it has ended. It may suit the adulterer to salve his or her conscience, but the risk is that it will destroy the innocent partner's trust. Truth is a dangerous weapon in the wrong hands, as Katharine Whitehorn wrote in her autobiography, *Selective Memory*: 'Those who tell a wife "for her own good" that her husband is cheating on her should probably be boiled in oil'.

Jealousy is not always about sex, of course. One person may be jealous of the other's friends, and complain that too much time is spent with them. It is not so much that the aggrieved party wants to be included, rather that they feel resentful about the time spent with people they don't like or have nothing in common with. 'You've got time for everyone except me,' is the cry of the neglected partner. For other couples, the golf course or the shopping mall stands in for mistress or lover. The golfer Gary Player was quoted as saying: 'It's a marriage. If I had to choose between my wife and my putter, well, I'd miss her.'

Couples can also find their relationship faltering because one of them has to work long, anti-social hours or because one or both of their extended families are too demanding. It's all too easy to create a space within a marriage that a third person may step into.

The problem all these cases have in common, it seems, is a breakdown of communication, caused often as not by a couple not seeing enough of each other. Try going out on a date together once in a while, as in the early days of courting (a good old-fashioned word for a good old-fashioned activity). If there are reasons not to go out, such as the lack of a babysitter, stay in for a 'night out', switch off the computer, do the candlelit dinner with all the trimmings or get a great takeaway and watch a DVD. It's a cliché but it works.

For a few, the cure for marital discontent is the very opposite of spending more time together. Husband and wife sometimes need a break. The idea is that they will miss each other when they're apart, and remember why they fell in love in the first place. It's a risky assumption. When a friend, feeling suffocated by her marriage, persuaded her husband that they both 'needed their own space' for a while, it turned out to be a big mistake. He was wounded by what felt to him like rejection, and while he was in this vulnerable state, along came another, delightful woman, only too willing to share her space with him. When they moved in together, his first wife realised her mistake, too late.

Career Rivalry

Some people just can't help competing with their partner, either socially or professionally, and it is jealousy, not of an outsider, but of their own partner's success that gnaws away inside them. They could be investment bankers, writers, brain surgeons, whatever... In Lionel Shriver's novel *Double Fault*, they happen to be tennis players. The heroine, Willy, confesses her jealousy, 'I hate it, you come home and you've won another big match and this anger rises in my throat like heartburn.'

Interviewed in *The Times*, Lionel Shriver said, 'It became a destructive element in my own life and I decided to write about it... You're married, you're supposed to be nice to each other, you're supposed to wish each other well... The problem is if one of you is doing crap, and the other is a high flyer, you're living in different worlds. Different emotional worlds, different social worlds and people are treating you differently.' She and her partner, both writers, lived in Belfast. Their fights were not overtly about their competitive careers, but (they are both Americans) about politics in Northern Ireland. Underlying the political rows was a personal, professional rivalry. Then, she says, she grew up. 'I started to get clued up on what it means to be somebody's partner and that you really root for them and they need that… You only get ill-wishing and competitiveness from the person on the losing end.'

Rivalry between partners is a fairly obvious problem when they share the same profession, but it can also be a problem if one is more successful in general than the other. In a horrifying case reported in the *Daily Telegraph*, Paul, aged 31, pleaded guilty to murdering his fiancée. Soon after they set up house together, 'tensions began to surface over his untidiness and her more ambitious outlook. While he held a number of low-paid jobs, she was progressing in her career and talked of travelling the world.' Their relationship deteriorated, and rows became more and more frequent until one evening he (who had a history of violence) lost his temper and strangled her.

Such an extreme case is obviously rare, but if there are feelings of bitterness about a partner's achievements, the cure is to be aware of feelings and convert them into pride in that success, and realise it could never have been achieved without loving support.

Forgive and Forget

> *Dear Princess Bibesco,*
> *I am afraid you must stop writing these little love*
> *letters to my husband while he and I live together.*

It's one of the things which are not done in our world.

You are very young. Won't you ask your husband to explain to you the impossibility of such a situation.

Please do not make me have to write to you again. I do not like scolding people and simply hate having to teach them manners.
Yours sincerely,
Katherine Mansfield
Letter written in 1921

A friend who caught her husband in bed with an old flame said it gave them both the impetus they needed to sort out their marital problems. He cut down on alcohol, they both attended counselling and their relationship is much stronger as a result.

Would that we could all be so mature and forgiving. Some people find it terribly difficult to forgive; and it can be equally difficult, for the one who has strayed, to accept forgiveness. A wife explains, 'Six months ago, I found out my husband was having an affair. He ended it immediately and hasn't seen the woman since, but I still feel terrible about it. He's very sorry and has promised never to hurt me again. I believe him, and still love him desperately, but I can't stop thinking about it.'

It is the same for some men, too: 'My wife had an affair and we haven't really got over it. I've forgiven her but I don't trust her any more. However, time is a great healer and I'm hoping we can eventually recover completely.'

Six months is not a long recovery period. The shock of discovery is usually followed by anger, sadness, confusion and sometimes embarrassment. The feelings must be worked through in their own time. It can't be rushed. So the 'guilty' partner shouldn't expect instant, total forgiveness, and the 'innocent' one should not expect their wounds to heal immediately. The 'innocent' partner should also accept some of the responsibility; the conditions in which infidelity occurs are often created by both parties.

The End of the Affair

> *Both my marriages were failures! Number*
> *one departed, and number two stayed.*
> **Gustav Mahler (1860-1911)**

When an affair becomes an excuse to end a marriage, the marriage was probably rocky already. For most couples divorce is not the inevitable outcome of an affair. Nor is it usually the desired outcome. People have affairs for all sorts of reasons and wanting to marry the new lover is not necessarily one of them.

Much as we may wish it were otherwise, however, there

will always be marriages that fail. To end a marriage is an agonising decision, and one which today is sometimes too lightly taken. Consider the way Anna Karenina's brother, Stiva Oblonsky, puts the case for divorce to her and then to her husband, scarcely realising the full complexities of the situation the couple actually find themselves in.

'Now the question is — can you go on living with your husband? Do you wish it? Does he wish it?'

'I don't know, I don't know at all.'

'But you said yourself that you can't endure him.'

'No, I didn't say so. I take it back. I don't know anything, I can't tell.'

'Yes, but let . . .'

'You can't understand. I feel I'm flying headlong over some precipice, but ought not to save myself. And I can't.'

'Never mind, we'll hold something out and catch you. I understand you, understand that you can't take it on yourself to express your wishes, your feelings.'

'There's nothing, nothing I wish . . . except for it to be all over.'

'But he sees that and knows it. Do you really suppose it weighs on him any less than on you? You're wretched, he's wretched, and what good can come of it? While a divorce would solve everything.' Oblonsky got out at last, not without difficulty *expressing his central idea, and looked at her significantly.*

She made no reply, and shook her cropped head in dissent. But from the look on her face, suddenly illuminated with its old beauty, he saw that if she did not desire this it was because it seemed to her unattainable happiness.

[Oblonsky later brings up the subject with Anna's husband, Karenin]

'To my way of thinking, what's essential in your case is to be on a new basis with each other. And that can only be done by both sides having their freedom.'

'Divorce,' Karenin interrupted with aversion.

'Yes, I imagine that divorce — yes, divorce,' repeated Oblonsky, reddening. 'From every point of view that is the most sensible solution for a couple who find themselves in the position you are in. What else can they do if they find life impossible together? It is a thing that may always happen.'

Karenin sighed heavily and closed his eyes.

'There is only one point to be considered: does either party wish to marry again? If not, it is very simple,' said Oblonsky, by degrees losing his embarrassment.

Karenin, his face drawn with emotion, muttered something to himself and made no reply. What appeared so simple to Oblonsky, he had thought over thousands and thousands of times, and, far from being simple, it all seemed to him utterly impossible. An action for divorce, with the details of which he was now acquainted, appeared to him out of the question, because his feelings of self-respect and his regard for religion forbade his pleading guilty to a fictitious act of adultery, and still less could he allow his wife, forgiven and beloved by him, to be exposed and put to shame. Divorce seemed to him impossible also on other still more weighty grounds.

In the event of a divorce, what would become of his son...

'Oh God, Oh God! How have I deserved this?' thought Karenin.

Anna Karenina, Leo Tolstoy (1873)

If it seems that a relationship is on the verge of breaking down, it's worth drawing back from the brink to consider the whole thing constructively. The questions to ask are not the obvious ones that spring to mind, such as 'Whose fault is it?'; 'What did I do wrong?' or 'How could he/she do that to me?' It's more constructive to think about the good things in the relationship – what attracted the couple to each other in the first place? What and who has changed? Have thoughts and feelings really altered so very much? Why? Have there been bad outside influences?

Prince Charles famously said 'whatever "love" means', when talking to the press about his engagement to Princess Diana. He may not have been a model husband but he might have had a point that being 'in love' may not be enough to sustain a marriage. The conventional idea is that being passionately 'in love' doesn't last, and deeper, more permanent, though less glamorous love develops over the years. We can be in love with someone we don't like very much, but for a long-term relationship to succeed we do need to like each other. We can consciously decide to love someone; and we can also decide to stop loving them. The one thing we can't do successfully is change someone. However, they can sometimes change themselves if they want it enough.

SIR PETER TEAZLE: …We shall now be the happiest couple.

LADY TEAZLE: And never differ again?

SIR PETER: No, never – though at the same time, indeed, my dear Lady Teazle, you must watch your temper very seriously; for in all our little quarrels, my dear, if you recollect, my love, you always began first.

LADY TEAZLE: I beg your pardon, my dear Sir Peter: indeed, you always gave the provocation.

SIR PETER: Now, see, my angel! Take care – contradicting isn't the way to keep friends.

LADY TEAZLE: Then, don't you begin it, my love!

SIR PETER: There now! You – you are going on. You don't perceive, my life, that you are just doing the very thing that you know always makes me angry.

LADY TEAZLE: Nay, you know if you will be angry without any reason, my dear –

SIR PETER: There! Now you want to quarrel again.

LADY TEAZLE: No, I'm sure I don't but, if you will be so peevish –

Sir Peter: There now! Who begins first?

LADY TEAZLE: Why, you, to be sure I said nothing – but there's no bearing your temper.

SIR PETER: No, no, madam: the fault's in our own temper. [The argument continues]

The School for Scandal
Richard Brinsley Sheridan (1777)

10
FIGHT THE GOOD FIGHT

We see how few matrimonies there be without chidings, brawlings, tauntings, repentings, bitter cursings, and fightings.
'On the State of Matrimony', *Book of Homilies* (1571)

I have never understood this liking for war. It panders to instincts already well catered for within the scope of any respectable domestic establishment.
Alan Bennett

A marriage without arguments would be unreal and, if we agreed with each other all the time, life would be quite dull. Andrew G. Marshall, relationship counsellor and author, wrote in *The Times* that 'a good argument is the most intimate thing that you can have with your partner.

It is passionate, it clears the air, brings all the hidden hurts into the open and offers the prospect of real change.'

But there are good ways and bad ways to argue, and different people have different ideas about what is acceptable. One partner's rational discussion is the other's acrimonious row.

Why Fight?

You could start an argument in an empty house, you.
Caption to a photograph by David Roberts in 'How We Are Now' exhibition at Tate Britain.

In the early stages of marriage, people often discover character traits that don't fit their romantic image of each other. The journalist Julie Burchill wrote that 'a cynic should never marry an idealist. For the cynic, marriage represents the welcome end of romantic life, with all its agony and ecstasy. But for the idealist, it is only the beginning'.

A critical partner
There was no denying that Dorothea was as

virtuous and lovely a young lady as he could have obtained for a wife; but a young lady turned out to be something more troublesome than he had conceived. She nursed him, she read to him, she anticipated his wants, and was solicitous about his feelings; but there had entered into the husband's mind the certainty that she judged him... it seemed like a betrayal. The young creature who had worshipped him with perfect trust had quickly turned into the critical wife; and early instances of criticism and resentment had made an impression which no tenderness and submission afterwards could remove. To his suspicious interpretation Dorothea's silence now was a suppressed rebellion; a remark from her which he had not in any way anticipated was an assertion of conscious superiority; her gentle answers had an irritating cautiousness in them.

Middlemarch, **George Eliot (1871)**

As with the case of Casaubon and Dorothea in *Middlemarch*, the reality of married life can bring with it certain irritations caused by nothing more than someone's personal style or failure to carry out a promised chore. We're forced to nag our partner, and we don't like the image of ourselves as a nag. Neither does the partner. With both people tired and on a short fuse, an argument develops.

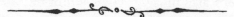

Things at home are crossways, and Betsey and I are
out....
We arg'd the thing at breakfast, we arg'd the thing
at tea,
And the more we arg'ed the question, the more we
didn't agree.
William Carleton (1794-1869)

Familiar metaphors give a clue about different styles of argument. We talk about winning and losing an argument as if it were at best a game, and at worst a war. Indeed G.K. Chesterton wrote that 'marriage is an adventure, like going to war.' A 'shouting match' can seem like a contest in which the one who shouts loudest will always win. In that game, however, a canny player can wrong-foot an opponent who raises his voice, simply by saying quietly, 'There's no need to shout'.

Marriage is like life in this — that it is a field of
battle, and not a bed of roses.
Robert Louis Stevenson (1850-94)

Then there are 'blazing' rows when one or both of the participants 'flare up' and become 'incandescent with rage'. The phrases 'I have a bone to pick with you' and 'bone of contention' conjure up a picture of two snarling terriers worrying at the same bone, neither of them prepared to let go. Even if the metaphorical bone is eventually buried, there's a strong chance that sooner or later it will be dug up and worried over again.

Some couples act out a parent/child relationship every time they argue. One partner plays the child, sulking, blaming and being obstinate. The other is the parent, condescending, criticising and telling the 'child' off.

If couples regularly have the same old arguments, they are probably both equally to blame and are not really arguing about who should have renewed the car insurance. They are tired and hormonal and worried about something at work. In short, they are spoiling for a fight and there's nobody else around to take their bad temper out on. We are deaf to the shrillness developing in our voice and once the argument is in full flood, we keep it going to protect our pride, to cover up feelings of guilt, and to avoid saying sorry. It hardly matters who initiates the argument, the result is the same: 'We're having a normal disagreement,' a husband explains, 'and suddenly, out of the blue, it escalates and things are said that are hard to draw back from. You do, eventually, of course, but the period of sulking can seem interminable.'

It destroys one's nerves to be amiable every day to the same human being.

Benjamin Disraeli (1804–81)

Most marital arguments are about money, sex, work, children and housework, roughly in that order. They are seldom about religion, politics, music, literature, or any great issue outside the home. That's why having a row is known as 'having a domestic'. Although I did find one couple whose worst row to date was about whether there could be a universal definition of 'Art'.

She says

It's always money problems: who should pay which bill, whose fault is the overdraft, why we can't earn more?

♥

I sometimes have a go at him for doggedly pursuing his own interests without enough thought for the rest of the family. His lack of help round the house is another on-going annoyance and I can't help nagging him about it.

♥

Things really erupt when I criticise his driving.

♥

*We argue about rules for the children, and parenting in
general.*

♥

*What drives me up the wall is his interference in what
I think of as my department: if we need a new carpet or
curtains I'm not allowed to choose them myself, and as his
taste is different from mine we have endless bad-tempered
arguments and end up with something neither of us
particularly likes. I really envy wives whose husbands
give them a free rein with the décor.*

He says

*We argue about which of us does the most cooking,
shopping, washing, house organising and tidying, child
and grandchild support, and holiday research.*

♥

*It's bridge, bridge and bridge again, at the card table,
in the car on the way home, bridge in bed, and sometimes
bridge at breakfast next day. She might be right, I
never should have led my king of diamonds. So what?*

♥

*I wouldn't say we argue much, it's more bickering, always
about the same domestic trivia.*

♥

*What to have for dinner when friends come is always an
issue. She has a happy-go-lucky idea that it's us they come
for, not our food, so pasta and a bottle of cheap wine will
do. Anyone would think we were all still students. I like to*

spoil people a bit — cook something special for them, and push the boat out as far as the wine is concerned.

We had a blazing row when she ate five of my Extra Strong mints in ten minutes.

It's best not to bottle up gripes, however trivial. Talking about them is good practice for arguing without loss of temper, a useful rehearsal for when the big issues come up. If, as often happens, there is a more serious hidden agenda, it can float to the surface and be dealt with.

In the following extract from Arnold Bennett's 1916 novel *These Twain*, Edwin kids himself that the row with his wife is about her moving the furniture. But the hidden agenda is about who is in control in this particular marriage.

[Hilda has moved the furniture in the drawing room without asking her husband Edwin. Furious, he has moved it back again while she was out.]

'Edwin,' she exclaimed very passionately, in a thick voice, quite unlike her usual clear tones, as she surveyed the furniture, 'this is really too much!'

'It's war, this is!' thought Edwin.

He was afraid; he was even intimidated by her anger; but he did not lose his courage... An in-

wardly feverish but outwardly calm vindictive desperation possessed him. He and she would soon know who was the stronger.

At the same time he said to himself:

'I was hasty. I ought not to have acted in such a hurry. Before doing anything I ought to have told her quietly that I intended to have the last word as regards furniture in this house. I was within my rights in acting at once, but it wasn't very clever of me, clumsy fool!'

Aloud he said, with a kind of self-conscious snigger:

'What's too much?'

Hilda went on:

'You simply make me look a fool in my own house, before my own son and the servants.'

'You've brought it on yourself,' said he fiercely. 'If you will do these idiotic things you must take the consequences. I told you I didn't want the furniture moved, and immediately my back's turned you go and move it. I won't have it, and so I tell you straight.'....

'You're a brute,' she continued, not heeding him, obsessed by her own wound. 'You're a brute!' She said it with terrifying conviction. 'Everybody knows it. Didn't Maggie warn me? You're a brute and a bully'...

'I think you ought to apologise to me,' she blubbered. 'Yes, I really do.'

'Why should I apologise to you? You moved the furniture against my wish. I moved it against

yours. That's all. You began. I didn't begin. You want everything your own way. Well, you won't have it.'

She blubbered once more: 'You ought to apologise to me.'

And then she wept hysterically.

He meditated sourly, harshly. He had conquered. The furniture was as he wished, and it would remain so. The enemy was in tears, shamed, humiliated… He did not mind apologising to her, if an apology would give her satisfaction. He was her superior in moral force, and naught else mattered.

'I don't think I ought to apologise,' he said with a slight laugh. 'But if you think so I don't mind apologising. I apologise. There!' He dropped into an easy chair.

To him it was as if he had said: 'You see what a magnanimous chap I am.'

She tried to conceal her feelings, but she was pleased, flattered, astonished. Her self-respect returned to her rapidly.

'Thank you,' she murmured, and added: 'It was the least you could do.'

At her last words he thought: 'Women are incapable of being magnanimous.'
[They kiss and make up.]
These Twain, Arnold Bennett (1916)

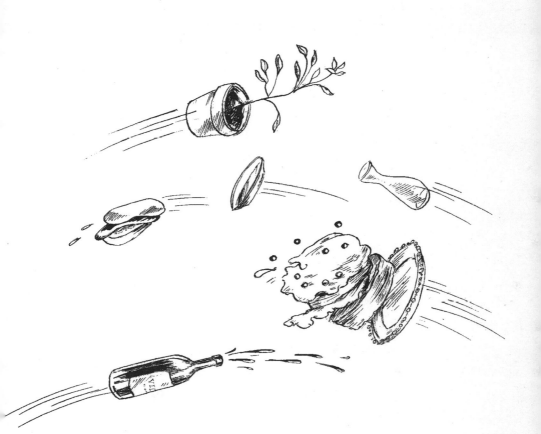

Missiles vary from cushions to cabbages to pot plants
and mobile phones...

Coming to Blows

For many years, the family were quite seriously prepared for Uncle Archie to murder Aunt Edith one day, and prepared, if he did, to go into the witness box on his behalf and swear that he did it under unendurable provocation.

Blue Remembered Hills, Rosemary Sutcliffe (1985)

It seems remarkable in a way that, even under great provocation, rows seldom become physical. Violence is always inexcusable, of course, but even in our usually harmonious household, goaded beyond endurance, I've been known to vent my spleen on inanimate objects. I once threw a frozen pat of butter at my husband's head. My aim being poor, the butter flew straight through the (fortunately open) kitchen window. I'm sure the provocation was great, but 40 years on, neither of us can remember what it was.

Women express their annoyance in the first place by rattling dishes and slamming doors. Dishes are apt to break when rattled. Broken to fragments and slammed into the dust bin, they also serve as a protest against the unfairness of the world.

[272]

The odd plate or saucer would mean no more than that, but the breaking of Wedgwood or Spode is something different. It reveals that you are behaving childishly, that you know your behaviour is childish, that you are punishing yourself like a child and using a childish form of punishment...
You go on to punish yourself and others until such time as you recover.

Mrs Parkinson's Law, C. Northcote Parkinson (1968)

Other missiles I've heard about vary from cushions (the soft option) to a cabbage and once, a hot dog which missed the husband and hit the baby. What else? A Christmas goose; a bucket of water; a vase, a fruit bowl, glasses, and two mobile phones; a plant in a pot ('I really regretted it when I was on my knees afterwards, trying to get the compost out of the carpet'); and a wedding ring ('I threw it in the bin because I felt he was throwing our relationship away, but he dug it out afterwards').

Mr and Mrs Cherry Owen, in their Donkey Street room that is bedroom, parlour, kitchen, and scullery, sit down to last night's supper of onions boiled in their overcoats and broth of spuds and bacon rind and leeks and bones.

MRS CHERRY OWEN: See that smudge on the wall by the picture of Auntie Blossom? That's where you threw the sago.
[Cherry Owen laughs with delight]
MRS CHERRY OWEN: You only missed me by an inch.
CHERRY OWEN: I always miss Auntie Blossom too.

Under *Milk Wood*, Dylan Thomas (1954)

Fight or Flight?

There are those who simply love arguing. They relish a chance to exercise their wit as well as their muscular jaws, and find it hard to understand that others dread arguments because they are not very articulate and cannot so easily marshall their points and express them.

'You are old,' said the youth, 'and your jaws are too weak
*   For anything tougher than suet;*
Yet you finished the goose, with the bones and the beak —
*   Pray, how did you manage to do it?'*

'In my youth,' said his father, 'I took to the law,

And argued each case with my wife;
And the muscular strength, which it gave to my
jaw,
   Has lasted the rest of my life.'

Alice's Adventures in Wonderland, Lewis
Carroll (1865)

According to temperament, an arguer's style will fall, broadly speaking, into one of two categories. The fighter tends to bring up controversial issues and, having started a fight, jumps at the chance to show off his or her arguing skills, sometimes getting more carried away than the trivial subject of the argument merits. 'What's the point of getting wound up about rotating food in the freezer?' says a wife married to a fighter 'Life's too short.'

Another wife, herself a fighter, says, 'If something needs saying, it always has to be me that says it. He would rather sweep everything under the carpet.' Sweeping problems under the carpet is what the second category of person does. Non-confrontational by nature, they prefer flight to fight.

To use a cricketing metaphor, the partner who brings up an issue is the bowler. The batsman responds either by blocking the ball (avoiding a row) or hitting it for six (engaging in a full-scale argument). If both partners are by nature fighters, the row will blaze for a short time and be resolved; the batsman will be clean bowled or will hit so many boundaries that the bowler gives in.

If one partner is a fighter and the other flees, however, issues can smoulder on for days or weeks. The battle will probably end in a draw, although the passive partner can sometimes win just by walking quietly out of the room. Storming out of the house, on the other hand, is an aggressive move and not to be recommended. It's hard to come back without losing face.

Most domestic arguments need to be resolved, or no decisions would ever get taken. Remember that agreeing to disagree, civilised and amiable as it may seem, may only lead to both partners withdrawing into more and more separate lives.

To Sulk or to Rant?

Most people, sulkers included, feel it's better to rant than to sulk; a good rant gets the poison out of the system and brings the conflict into the open where it can be dealt with. All agree that, after a quarrel, it's best to end on a positive note and not to let the sun go down on bad feeling. Ranting has the advantage of being essentially short term. Sulking carries on – and on and on.

It's true that it can take an hour or so to calm a ranter down, but it may take days to coax a sulker back out of their shell. Here are some comments from both camps.

It's better to rant because...
When he sulks I just have no idea what it's about and the

only response I can get out of him is 'If you don't know, I'm not going to explain'. Am I supposed to be telepathic?

♥

He sulks and I hate it because it doesn't achieve anything apart from making him more wound up and making me miserable. It's emotional blackmail really. I'm supposed to feel guilty but he won't tell me why.

♥

Sulking is no fun for the sulker and only makes the sulked-against person feel self-righteous.

♥

Ranting gets better results; at least you know what the other person's feeling pissed off about.

♥

I'm a world-class sulker and can keep it up indefinitely, creating a bad atmosphere for days on end. I'm not proud of it, it's just the way I am, and I wish I wasn't. I sit inside a black cloud of festering resentment and I can't fight my way out of it.

It's better to sulk because...
Ranting and raving without thinking about what you're saying can do a lot of damage; you may say something really wounding. You might give anything to unsay it, but once it's out, it's out.

♥

Ranting is a waste of energy, and should only be used when volcanic explosion is appropriate (that is, never).

[277]

How to Have a Civilised Argument

To keep your marriage brimming
With love in the loving cup,
Whenever you're wrong, admit it,
Whenever you're right shut up.
Ogden Nash (1902-71)

Most arguments need never occur in the first place and it's pointless for them to be repeated again and again. When, before writing this chapter, I sat down with my husband to discuss what subjects we argue about, we found there were surprisingly few: we've been digging up the same old bones and worrying at them on and off for 47 years.

One sensible bit of advice I was once given is that bad temper is infectious, but luckily, niceness is infectious too, so if one of the two remembers this, smiles and says something pleasant, harmony is soon restored.

Another way to avoid arguments is to make allowances for annoying character tics. If it drives one person crazy that the other one is always ten minutes late, simply tell the slowcoach that the party starts at 8.20 not 8.30. On the other hand, if pathological punctuality is the problem, give up hovering by the front door looking at a watch. And if you are the one who is prone to start new projects with great enthusiasm and leave them unfinished, don't wait to be nagged yet again about the unhemmed curtains; get out the sewing box and hem them.

In my experience, men hate to hear women criticising other women. They are also variously enraged by our apparent lack of logic (in other words, our intuition or lateral thinking), by our need for constant reassurance that we are loved and, above all, by crying. When a man's unreasonableness reduces a woman to tears, to him it's not weeping, it's blubbing or turning on the waterworks, and it doesn't wring his heart.

For worse, he says

She always interrupts. Instead of listening to me she jumps in with some point she's been saving up.

♥

My wife wants to win every argument. She cuts in on what I'm saying, raises her voice to overpower mine, and uses scorn, contempt, and sarcasm.

For better, he says

I steer clear of an argument by reassuring her, 'you have a right to your opinion'. This implies that I, too, have a right to my opinion.

♥

We have no problem saying sorry to each other when we're wrong and neither of us gloats after arguments, whoever 'won'. If you can avoid sulking, and don't go to sleep

*harbouring a grudge, and can genuinely forget what went
wrong yesterday, you'll be OK.*

For worse, she says
*His logic is relentless and he always wins against my more
intuitive approach.*

♥

*I'm non-adversarial and not good at arguing, whereas he
is confident and very persistent in expressing his views. It's
no good me saying 'You're wrong but I can't explain why',
so he always wins and I surrender and simmer.*

♥

*When he's in the wrong he never admits it till a couple of
days later.*

♥

For better, she says
*Whatever happens, we somehow always manage to keep a
channel of communication open.*

♥

*I never bother to fight the minor battles. I'm keeping
my powder dry for a major issue.*

♥

*We don't argue often and when tempers do get lost, we
just have cooling-off non-speaks for a bit and are soon
back to normal.*

♥

Rules of Engagement

Don't

cross-examine a partner — it's not a court of law.

prevaricate. Give straight answers.

try and enlist the sympathy of a third party,
especially not a parent.

belittle a partner in front of friends, however wittily.
It erodes self-esteem and embarrasses the friends.

call a partner names.

interrupt.

argue in front of the children and especially not if
their friends are there.

treat an argument as an opportunity to list all a
partner's character failings.

argue over trivia.

swear or shout.

argue after a drink.

try and score points. It's a discussion, not a
competition.

waste time arguing about the way you argue: 'you
never let me finish' etc.

Do

remember you love each other really.

laugh to defuse the argument. One couple keeps two water pistols handy to use when an argument gets out of hand. It works because neither of them can keep a straight face.

save serious arguments for a walk. Eye contact can be avoided and the exercise helps release tension.

look for the hidden agenda; the argument you are having may not be the real one.

let the partner have their say, even if it requires superhuman patience.

ask questions, but in a neutral, not hostile way.

Avoid using incantatory words or phrases, such as 'Now look what you made me do', 'Why don't you...?' 'You never... you always...' and especially 'You're just like your mother'. 'I told you so' and its variations: 'I knew this would happen' and 'I could have told you that would happen' to which the answer is 'Then why didn't you?' are all red card phrases.

Kiss and Make Up

29 May 1897
The Progressive Review

My dearest Wiffie
I am very wretched for this morning, I forgot my-
self — why? I do not know, & would give anything
to undo it. This is a special day with us too. But I
have been sending telegrams all morning & think
I have been receiving them. Ever, my dearie, your
own unsatisfactory man.

X X X X

Letter from Ramsay MacDonald to
Margaret MacDonald

By far the easiest way to stop fighting is to see the funny side. Laugh at the absurdity of the situation. But, of course, don't laugh at a partner. If neither person is in a laughing mood, try kissing and making up. Swallow your pride; there's no point in trying to maintain the moral high ground — there is none, and if we imagine there is and that we are on it, it's pointless saying to ourselves, 'I'm in the right and he has to apologise'. If he does, he almost certainly won't mean it.

For a row to end, someone has to admit they were wrong, and it might as well be you. And yet strangely, if we know in our heart of hearts we were wrong, the words 'I was wrong and you were right' stick in the throat. Say it with fingers crossed, if it helps. Or go halfway, with 'I may have been wrong and you may have been right'. Offering a compromise can give us a little glow of pleasure at our own magnanimity. Whereas, not admitting that we were at least a little bit at fault will make us feel mean and resentful and prolong the row. A sheepish 'Sorry!' (not a scowling 'Sorreeee'), a smile if we can manage it and a tentative hug, and it's over. Painless, really.

The contradictory couple

The contradictory couple agree in nothing but contradiction. They return home from Mrs Bluebottle's dinner-party, each in an opposite corner of the coach,
and do not exchange a syllable until they have been seated for at least 20 minutes by the fireside at home, when the gentleman, raising his eyes from the stove, all at once breaks silence:

'What a very extraordinary thing it is,' says he, 'that you WILL contradict, Charlotte!'

'I contradict!' cries the lady, 'but that's just like you.'

'What's like me?' says the gentleman sharply.

'Saying that I contradict you,' replies the lady.

'Do you mean to say that you do NOT contradict me?' retorts the gentleman. 'Do you mean to say that you have not been contradicting me the whole of this day?'…

Swallow your pride; there's no point in trying to
maintain the moral high ground — there is none.

'I mean to tell you nothing of the kind,' replies the lady quietly; 'when you are wrong, of course I shall contradict you.'

During this dialogue the gentleman has been taking his brandy-and-water on one side of the fire, and the lady, with her dressing-case on the table, has been curling her hair on the other. She now lets down her back hair, and proceeds to brush it; preserving at the same time an air of conscious rectitude and suffering virtue, which is intended to exasperate the gentleman — and does so.

'I do believe,' he says, taking the spoon out of his glass, and tossing it on the table, 'that of all the obstinate, positive, wrong-headed creatures that were ever born, you are the most so, Charlotte.'

'Certainly, certainly, have it your own way, pray. You see how much I contradict you,' rejoins the lady.

'Of course, you didn't contradict me at dinner-time — oh no, not you!' says the gentleman.

'Yes, I did,' says the lady.

'Oh, you did,' cries the gentleman; 'you admit that?'

'If you call that contradiction, I do,' the lady answers; 'and I say again, Edward, that when I know you are wrong, I will contradict you. I am not your slave.'

'Not my slave!' repeats the gentleman bitterly; 'and you still mean to say that in the Blackburns' new house there are not more than fourteen doors, including the door of the wine-cellar!'

'I mean to say,' retorts the lady, beating time with her hair-brush on the palm of her hand, 'that in that house there are fourteen doors and no more.'

'Well then — ' cries the gentleman, rising in despair, and pacing the room with rapid strides. 'By G—, this is enough to destroy a man's intellect, and drive him mad!'

Sketches of Young Couples, Charles Dickens (1855)

TO MY DEAR AND
LOVING HUSBAND

If ever two were one, then surely we.
If ever man were lov'd by wife, then thee;
If ever wife was happy in a man,
Compare with me, ye women if you can.
I prize thy love more than whole Mines of gold,
Or all the riches that the East doth hold.

My love is such that Rivers cannot quench,
Nor ought but love from thee, give recompense.
Thy love is such I can no way repay,
The heavens reward thee manifold I pray.
Then while we live, in love lets so persever,
That when we live no more, we may live ever.

Anne Bradstreet (1650)

11
HAPPILY EVER AFTER

This, the final chapter, is a celebration of successful and happy marriages. It goes without saying that no two marriages are the same, just as no two people are the same in character and temperament. A marriage can be tempestuous or calm, earnest or light-hearted, extrovert or introvert. We can marvel at unlikely partnerships. 'I can't think what he sees in her,' we say; 'or she in him'; and we wonder what it is that makes the couple so contented with each other. In this book I've tried to analyse some of the elements that lead to that contentment. Some have been fairly self-evident; others may have seemed contradictory.

Happy Talk

May 5th [1948] Ralph to London to the dentist.
I have sprained my ankle so cannot go with him,
but as the years pass I hate being parted from him
even for an hour or so; I feel only half a person by
myself, with one arm one leg and half a face...
Everything to Lose: Diaries 1945-60,
Frances Partridge

It's generally agreed that communication is one of the keys to a happy relationship, yet some of the most touching testimonials to marriage, like the passage from Frances Partridge's diaries quoted above, come from a generation much more reticent than ours about discussing their feelings. Anyone brought up in Britain during or between World Wars I and II learned a stoicism at odds with open displays of emotion, and communication between husband and wife was sometimes difficult.

Often he thought: My life did not begin until I
knew her.
She would like to hear this, he was sure, but he
did not know how to tell her... He needed to let
her know how deeply he felt her presence while

they were lying together during the night, as well as each morning when they awoke and in the evening when he came home. However, he could think of nothing appropriate.

As time went on she felt an increasing need for reassurance. Her husband had never been a demonstrative man, not even when they were first married; consequently she did not expect too much from him. Yet there were moments when she was overwhelmed by a terrifying, inarticulate need. One evening as she and he were finishing supper together, alone, the children having gone out, she inquired rather sharply if he loved her. She was surprised by her own bluntness and by the almost shrewish tone of her voice, because that was not the way she actually felt. She saw him gazing at her in astonishment; his expression said very clearly: Why on earth do you think I'm here if I don't love you? Why aren't I somewhere else? What in the world has got into you?

Mrs Bridge and Mr Bridge, Evan S. Connell, (1959)

———————⬦⬦⬦———————

In the 21st century, couples are less inhibited. They walk hand in hand and delight in telling how much they love each other — some chant the mantra 'love you, babe' when they wake up in the morning, when they leave for work, when they phone each other during the day, when they get home and last thing before falling asleep. One wife, happily married for many years, warns against allowing love-speak and kisses to become 'a doorstep ritual'. If your partner is run over by a bus, the fact that you went through the ritual may comfort you, but too frequent and routine usage makes it meaningless. 'It's more important,' she says, 'to give a spontaneous hug or peck on the cheek, an arm round your partner's shoulder, or a back rub whenever the spirit moves you. A compliment on your partner's appearance, cooking, or even driving, also never comes amiss.'

These small, attentive expressions of love are not trivial, although they may seem so compared to the less visible rapport that a couple can develop, enabling them to talk to each other without ever becoming bored, even after several decades together.

They had always been very close to each other, united by indistinguishably close bonds of love and intelligence. They had never ceased passionately to crave each other's company. They had never seriously quarrelled, never been parted, never doubted each other's complete honesty. A style of directness and truthfulness composed the particular gaiety of their lives. Their love had grown, nourished daily by the liveliness of their shared thoughts. They had grown together in mind and body and soul

as it is sometimes blessedly given to two people to do. They could not be in the same room without touching each other. They constantly uttered even their most trivial thoughts. Their converse passed through wit. Jest and reflection had been the language of their love.

Nuns and Soldiers, Iris Murdoch (1980)

On the other hand, in some long-lasting marriages, words become almost redundant. Husband and wife develop subtle codes to express their love, involving the catching of an eye, the ghost of a private smile or the brief touch of a hand. They sometimes begin or finish each other's sentences. 'One of the nicest things about living with someone,' says a wife, 'is each knowing what the other wants without having to ask. A telepathy has developed between us.' This telepathy cannot be established overnight, and the longer the marriage lasts, the more frequent and delightful it becomes.

Companionship

Modern descriptions of happy marriages on internet chatrooms emphasise the kind of closeness that comes from years of getting to know each other inside out.

He's definitely my best mate, and the only person I can

stand spending a lot of time with — everyone else gets on my nerves after a while. And I never cease to wonder how he puts up with me and my annoying ways and still loves me. We seem to fit each other like gloves.

♥

We've just celebrated our Silver Wedding, and I can honestly say that after 25 years we are closer and happier than we've ever been. We still make each other laugh, and can talk about anything and everything for hours. Of course we have our ups and downs and sometimes I could strangle him (and he me) but we'd be lost without each other.

♥

Above all, we're good friends. When shit hits the fan we just hang out together and sort it. Plus neither of us holds grudges for each other's mistakes, we do it, talk it over and it's gone. We do have an old style type of relationship: solid, he provides and supports, I hold the house and kids together, we pootle along with few ups and downs. The passion / sex has highs and slumps, but our friendship carts us through the worst bits with good humour.

November 2. I spent the evening quietly with Carrie, of whose company I never tire. We had a most pleasant chat about the letters on 'Is Marriage a Failure?' It has been no failure in our case. In talking over our own happy experiences, we never

noticed that it was past midnight.
Diary of a Nobody, George and Weedon Grossmith (1892)

The companionship of marriage can grow stronger and closer through the years, and as well as enhancing the time you spend together, it extends into the parts of your life spent away from your partner, so that you make a mental note of anecdotes and incidents from the time you spend with the children or in your work place, to share at the end of the day.

When I get back from work she's full of funny chat about her day, and it helps me unwind.

♥

He entertains me with news about what went on at work and who he saw at lunchtime — it's like a daily soap opera, and quite as good as anything on telly.

♥

I sort of actively look out for things that will make him laugh and save them for when we're alone together.

A happy marriage is a long conversation that always seems too short.
André Maurois (1885-1967)

The Best Medicine

The exchange of daily news is all the more satisfying when served up with a sense of humour. It's no accident that every ad in every lonely-hearts column makes 'gsoh' a primary requirement. Virtually everyone I spoke to, from newly-weds to veterans, put it at the top of their list: 'She can always make me laugh, specially when I don't feel like it,' 'He's such fun to be with,' 'We share jokes,' 'She's entertaining when we're with friends,' 'He has the gift of the gab.' 'There's a quirky synergy between us that means I can still, 25 years later, make him laugh so hard he almost chokes.'

Dare I say that today's young couples sometimes take their marital problems a little too solemnly? I don't think it's an exaggeration to say that laughter is the single most important ingredient in a happy marriage.

Looking Ahead

> *Grow old along with me!*
> *The best is yet to be...*
> **Rabbi Ben Ezra, Robert Browning**
> **(1864)**

Over the years I've sometimes doubted if Browning is right. My reasoning was – on balance it's been pretty good so far, it would surely be pushing our luck to think it could get any better. Many incidents in our 47 years of married life are described in this book, either openly or disguised. They include 'for worse' episodes as well as 'for better', some trivial, some serious. I've included them and the experiences of other real-life couples to show what a unique and wonderful thing marriage is, if you stay the course. Maddening as we find each other at times, as we have grown older our life together has gone on getting better. There's so much to look back on, but there's still a lot to look forward to. So perhaps the best really is still to come.

> ...*marriage is the water in which you swim, the land you live in: the habits, the assumptions you share about the future, about what's funny or deplorable, about the way the house is run — or should be; what Anthony Burgess called a whole civilization, a culture, 'a shared language of grunt and touch.'*
> **Selective Memory, Katharine Whitehorn (2007)**

ACKNOWLEDGEMENTS

Many friends have contributed to this book and I wish I could thank each of them individually by name. But I promised anonymity, so I must thank them collectively. It is their book as much as it is mine, and I thank them for being funny, wise, wistful, romantic, practical, intuitive – and generally confirming what I instinctively knew: that marriage is a good thing. The fact that I have never doubted it is due to my wonderful family. Thank you Rob, Sophy and Nick, Hugh and Marie and my grandchildren Chloe, Max, Oscar, Guy and Freddie.

This is my fourth book to be published by Short Books, and I could not wish for a more creative, efficient, cheerful and sympathetic team. Thank you Aurea Carpenter, Rebecca Nicolson, Emily Fox and Vanessa Webb. Thank you, Charlotte Thompson, for your skilful editing and Stephanie von Reiswitz for your witty and wonderful drawings.

I would like to thank to the following for permission to use copyright material: Rosemary A. Thurber and the Barbara Hogenson Agency for extracts from *Thurber Country* by James Thurber, Copyright © 1949; Curtis Brown on behalf of Katharine Whitehorn for extract from *Selective Memory* Copyright © Katharine Whitehorn 2007; Curtis Brown Group Ltd on behalf of Mary Soames for Winston and Clementine: *The Personal Letters of the Churchills* Copyright © Mary Soames 2001; Julian Fellowes for an extract from an magazine article; David Higham Associates for an extract from *Portraits and Prayers* by Gertrude Stein (Random House 1934) and for an extract from *Under Milk Wood* by Dylan Thomas (Penguin Classics 2000; The Estate of Georgette Heyer for extracts from *A Civil*